Who Am I, Lord?

Who Am I, Lord?

WHO AM I, LORD?

*Finding Your
Identity in Christ*

JOE HESCHMEYER

Our Sunday Visitor
Huntington, Indiana

Nihil Obstat
Msgr. Michael Heintz, Ph.D.
Censor Librorum

Imprimatur
✠ Kevin C. Rhoades
Bishop of Fort Wayne-South Bend
December 15, 2019

Our Sunday Visitor Publishing Division
Our Sunday Visitor, Inc.
200 Noll Plaza
Huntington, IN 46750
1-800-348-2440

ISBN: 978-1-68192-327-7 (Inventory No. T1998)
1. RELIGION—Christian Life—Personal Growth. 2. RELIGION—Christian Theology—Christology. 3. RELIGION—Christianity—Catholic.

eISBN: 978-1-68192-328-4
LCCN: 2019956578

Cover and interior design: Lindsey Riesen
Cover art: Christ Blessing/El Greco/Restored Traditions

PRINTED IN THE UNITED STATES OF AMERICA

*To Anna Heschmeyer, née Krestyn,
for showing me the power of
name changes and identity*

Table of Contents

INTRODUCTION
Who Are You?

It's 2008, and Sebastian Junger is near the border of Afghanistan and Pakistan, in an area known as "the Valley of Death." That's the name the twenty young men who make up Battle Company 2/503 have chosen for the Korangal Valley, a particularly bloody battleground in the Afghan war. Junger is embedded with the battalion as a journalist for *Vanity Fair*, but why are these other young men here? There was no draft that forced them to put their lives on the line, and the war in Afghanistan has entered its eighth year by this point. Why are these men risking their lives?

So Junger asks the men why they joined. Later, he would recount that while some of them listed 9/11 or a family history of military service, the "more thoughtful" men responded, "Well, I sorta thought it might make a man out of me."[1] Military service was, for these young men, a way of forming a "warrior identity." Junger points to this identity as the reason many military veterans expressed eagerness to return to combat, willing even to serve as civilian volunteers in the fight against ISIS:

> Their identity is now that of a warrior, and they don't know what they would be, or who they would be in civilian life. So they go back to combat because at least that's an identity that they like and that they're proud of. It's a lot harder to be proud of a civilian identity just because it's more mundane. I don't care what company

you're the president of, you're still not in a life-and-death situation. No matter how high up you rise in civilian life, you're still not doing something as intense as the lowest ranking grunt in a firefight. That identity, that warrior identity, is the thing I think they become psychologically dependent on.[2]

Why start a book on identity here? For several reasons. First, it points to the importance of the question. We can trace a direct line from the adoption of this "warrior" identity to the men later returning to life-or-death situations. Second, it is suggestive of the scope of the problem. The young men of Battle Company 2/503 are hardly the only ones trying to sort through these questions of identity. Pope Saint John Paul II suggests that "Who am I?" and "Where have I come from and where am I going?" are among "the fundamental questions which pervade human life," which every great religion and philosophy must try to answer:

These are the questions which we find in the sacred writings of Israel, as also in the Veda and the Avesta; we find them in the writings of Confucius and Lao-Tze, and in the preaching of Tirthankara and Buddha; they appear in the poetry of Homer and in the tragedies of Euripides and Sophocles, as they do in the philosophical writings of Plato and Aristotle. They are questions which have their common source in the quest for meaning which has always compelled the human heart. In fact, the answer given to these questions decides the direction which people seek to give to their lives.[3]

But our culture is failing to answer (and even to permit asking) these questions. As Junger points out, "This is probably the first society in history that actively discourages an intelligent conversation about what manhood should require of men."[4] Even this may be putting the problem too mildly. In the face of these universal, fundamental questions of human life, questions of life-and-death importance that shape the whole direction of our lives, our society has no answer except to say that there is no objective answer.

We can do better than this. That's what this book is all about.

Three Simple Ideas

This book is built upon three ideas so simple that we often fail to recognize them:

1. *You can't know how to behave unless you know who you are.* Action, in other words, is rooted in identity. To know what's expected of you in a certain situation, or what you ought to do, you must have a sense of who you are. Books and films, such as *The Bourne Identity*, are centered on this. Going through life without a clear, accurate sense of identity is dangerous. Once you know who you are, on the other hand, you know how to act.

To see the important connection between identity and action, consider a real-life case, such as Kate Middleton, who went from being a "commoner" to being royalty. Her transition in identity led to a transition in activity. British royalty follow a nuanced protocol that forbids autographs[5] and regulates even the order of dinner conversation ("the Queen begins by speaking to the person seated to her right. During the second course of the meal, she switches to the guest on her left").[6] You probably don't follow those rules, and you don't have to, just as Middleton didn't have to when she was single. But those rules are now important parts of her new, royal identity, and for good reasons.[7] A great many more rules and guidelines, such as the ban on the royals' taking selfies or wearing skimpy clothing, help to protect the image of the royal family.

Most of us have never undergone a change quite *that* dramatic. But for married readers, there may be something relatable. A great deal of the behavior you engaged in while single (from dating other people to leaving your socks lying around) may no longer be acceptable. You also likely have a number of obligations that you didn't have before. On the other hand, a whole range of behaviors, such as having sexual relations, living together, and having children, went from being sinful before marriage to positively encouraged after. Marriage created a new dimension of your identity, and with this change in identity came a change in what is and isn't morally acceptable. So, if you want to know how to behave, you first have to know who you are. You can't answer "What should I do?" without first being able to answer "Who am I?"

2. *You can't answer "Who am I?" without being able to answer "Am I created or an accident?"* Everything around you points to the fact that you were created, and designed, and have a purpose. Consider your appendix, the little two- to four-inch pouch nestled in your intestines. It baffled scientists for ages, since it doesn't seem to be necessary. If you remove someone's heart, that's going to kill him. If you remove his legs, that's going to impact the course of his life seriously. But if you remove the appendix, nothing seems to happen. For this reason, Charles Darwin confidently declared that "not only is it useless, but it is sometimes the cause of death."[8]

For 150 years, Darwin's view of the appendix as a "useless evolutionary artifact" was accepted nearly universally.[9] As recently as 2009, the biologist and "New Atheist" Jerry Coyne was still calling the appendix "the most famous" of the "many vestigial features proving that we evolved" and claiming that it "is simply the remnant of an organ that was critically important to our leaf-eating ancestors, but of no real value to us."[10] But even when Coyne wrote these words, scientists were beginning to realize that this was untrue. In 2007, researchers at Duke University proposed "that the appendix is designed to protect good bacteria in the gut. That way, when the gut is affected by a bout of diarrhea or other illness that cleans out the intestines, the good bacteria in the appendix can repopulate the digestive system and keep you healthy."[11] Further research has supported this theory. People without an appendix are more likely to suffer from particular infections. In 2016, scientists discovered that the lining of the appendix contains "a newly discovered class of immune cells known as innate lymphoid cells" that help to ward off bacteria and viruses, and experiments on mice confirmed that the animals without these cells were more prone to "pathological gut infection."[12] This isn't a unique story: other organs previously viewed as pointless evolutionary leftovers, such as the coccyx, are now recognized as having purposes we previously didn't understand.[13]

What's perhaps most striking about this discussion about the appendix and the coccyx is that scientists, researchers, and journalists are openly discussing the "design" and "purpose" of these organs. That's a remarkable, if tacit, admission, because you can't have design or purpose without a designer. As Richard Dawkins puts it, atheism posits that "the universe we observe has precisely the properties we should expect if there is, at bottom, no design, no purpose, no evil and no good, nothing but blind, pitiless indifference."[14] But we repeatedly see that that's not the case. Even Coyne (whose book boasts Dawkins' endorsement on the cover) speaks of what he considers the body's "imperfect design."[15] Whether you like or dislike the design, whether you fully understand it or not or consider it perfect or lacking, there's a whole world of difference between "imperfect design" and "random chance."

If I were to ask you about the "purpose" of the shape of spilled milk on the floor, you would rightly find the question baffling, even meaningless. It has no purpose; it's just a random accident. And so, it makes no sense to talk about the purpose of a particular part of the spill, any more than it makes sense to talk about the intention of the accident as a whole. But if I were to ask you about the purpose of the heart or the lungs, I'm sure you would have no trouble giving an explanation. We realize, on some level, that our bodies *aren't* random accidents. We can't escape recognizing that the body is designed with a purpose, and that the parts make sense — or when they initially don't, as with the appendix or the coccyx, it's probably we who are in the wrong. The point here is that no part of you is random and useless, even if it sometimes seems that way. That seems to suggest that *you're* not random and useless either; that you, like every part of your body, have a purpose. This is a crucial finding, because it starts to answer that question of identity. But it's only a beginning — we need to go a little deeper.

3. *If you want to understand your mission and why you were created, you need to get to know your Creator.* Once you recognize that you are created, the next question is "Who made me, and why?" There are many ways of trying to understand your purpose or design, but the single best one is to ask the Designer himself.

This is one of the reasons people interview authors — to try to understand their books better. Scholars can put forth their best interpretation about what a novel means, but that's just educated guesswork. To know for sure, you have to ask the author. Take Arthur Miller's 1953 play, *The Crucible*, a common staple of high school English classes across the United States. On the surface, it's "a story of the persecution of persons accused of witchcraft in Salem in 1692," as the *New York Times* described it in 1956.[16] But critics quickly speculated that it was really a thinly veiled critique of the "Red Scare" of their day, the Congressional attempt to root out prominent secret Communists. Miller had been active in Communist front groups in the 1940s and would be brought before the House Un-American Activities Committee (HUAC) in 1956, when he refused to "name names" of his associates.[17] So it stands to reason that *The Crucible* was a sort of response to HUAC and Senator Joe McCarthy. The problem was that "Arthur Miller kept a lot of things close to the vest" and "was always coy about divulging his total intentions [about the play] on-the-record."[18] Critics could suspect but couldn't really say for sure, until Miller finally broke his silence in 1996, in the *New Yorker* article "Why I Wrote 'The Crucible,'" in which he said: "In 1950, when I began to think of writing about the hunt for Reds in America, I was motivated in some great part by the paralysis that had set in among many liberals who, despite their discomfort with the inquisitors' violations of civil rights, were fearful, and with good reason, of being identified as covert Communists if they should protest too strongly."[19] The critics, in other words, had been right. But they couldn't really know if their speculations were correct until they heard from the author himself.

Sometimes the critical consensus is wrong. When an English professor wrote on behalf of his class to ask Flannery O'Connor if the central plot points of "A Good Man Is Hard to Find" had all been in the imagination of one of the characters, she replied that this interpretation was "about as far from my intentions as it could get to be. If it were a legitimate interpretation, the story would be little more than a trick and its interest would be simply for abnormal psychology. I am not interested in abnormal psychology. … My tone is not meant to be obnoxious. I am in a state of shock."[20] But how do we know if we're like the readers of *The Crucible*, who have accurately discerned the deeper meaning, or those of "A Good Man Is Hard to Find," who couldn't have been more wrong? Ultimately, only by listening to the author.

Getting Identity Wrong

What if we don't go to the author or take the trouble to sort out the deeper meaning of the questions of identity? It's not that we'll make it through life without answering the questions. Everyone, implicitly or explicitly, has to answer. But we'll arrive at false or superficial answers.

Two seemingly unrelated political trends point to the most common way we can answer identity questions badly. The first is the story of Facebook's gender experiments. Before February 2014, Facebook knew of only two genders. Users could choose either "male" or "female." But this was viewed as overly restrictive, so the company added fifty-four new options, such as "Two-Spirit," "Neutrois," "Genderqueer," and "Other."[21] These options proved to be too limiting, and so, by June, the company had partnered with LGBT advocacy organizations to come up with an additional twenty-one genders.[22] By the following February, the company gave up trying to keep up with the proliferation of genders, instead creating a choose-your-own-gender option for those with "custom genders."[23]

The second most common way we can answer identity questions badly is the role of "identity politics" as a (or perhaps *the*) critical force in electoral politics in the West. Francis Fukuyama, the political scientist perhaps most famous for his book *The End of History*, argues that "identity politics has become a master concept that explains much of what is going on in global affairs."[24] "Identity politics" (an admittedly amorphous term) is rooted in two premises. First, rather than seeking the well-being of your neighbor, you should be worried about "your group." As the 1977 Combahee River Collective Statement explains, "This focusing upon our own oppression is embodied in the concept of identity politics. We believe that the most profound and potentially most radical politics come directly out of our own identity, as opposed to working to end somebody else's oppression."[25] Of course, this raises a second question: What's "your group" or "your identity"? In the world of identity politics, you're defined by your race, or sex, or sexual orientation, or gender identity, or mental or physical disability, or some intersecting blend of those things. (Tellingly, the Combahee River Collective Statement was created by African-American feminists who didn't feel adequately represented by either the Black Power movement or the feminist movement). As Fukuyama recognizes, such a movement, in the long run, will serve only to divide people further and further, as it's an inherently tribalistic politics.

This also is one reason we have become obsessed with politics. Instead of a campaign cycle, everything seems to be permanently political. The political scientist Sheri Berman astutely observed:

> In the past, the Republican and Democratic parties attracted supporters with different racial, religious, ideological and regional identities, but gradually Republicans became the party of white, evangelical, con-

servative and rural voters, while the Democrats became associated with non-whites, non-evangelical, liberal and metropolitan voters.

This lining up of identities dramatically changes electoral stakes: previously if your party lost, other parts of your identity were not threatened, but today losing is also a blow to your racial, religious, regional and ideological identity.[26]

Fukuyama's fear is that identity politics means (or is coming to mean) that the difference between the two parties is not primarily in what they stand for, but in *whom* they stand for. In this way, answering the question of identity badly has helped to propel the breakup of civic societies across the globe.

Outside the realm of politics, we find the question answered badly in other ways. For example, we often seek our identities (and our validation and fulfillment) in relationships and in the praise of peers. As an example of the first case, take the person who needs to be constantly in a dating relationship. In its most extreme manifestations, this can become codependency. As Jo-Ann Krestan and Claudia Bepko note, "Loss of identity is precisely at the core of the dominant definitions of codependency," as the codependent person defines himself or herself simply in relation to another person.[27] As for seeking our identities in the praise of peers, a growing body of research explores the "effects of interpersonal relationships and digital-media use on adolescents' sense of identity," since they "are growing and entering a critical stage in which they find themselves seeking coherence and consistency in their sense of identity and increased clarity in their self-concepts," all while spending a shocking number of hours looking at screens and engaged in primarily digital interactions with their peers and with the world.[28] One consequence of the growing role of social media, as we shall see in chapter 6, involves skyrocketing rates of anxiety and depression.

Another example of answering the question of identity badly

is evident in the popularity of books such as Elizabeth Gilbert's *Eat, Pray, Love*, despite its being "narcissistic New Age reading." The author says vapid things such as "When you fill up your own skin with yourself, that alone becomes your offering."[29] (The book revolves around a woman's quest to "find herself" by divorcing her husband and traveling around the world to eat Italian food, explore Indian religion, and have a steamy romance in Bali).

On the surface, there seems to be little in common between how many genders Facebook decides to include, and what a Black Feminist group had to say about political activism in 1977, and why it's hard to be single sometimes, and how spending a lot of time on social media can make you feel low. But a thread ties together all of these things and many others: They're all related to our constant effort to discover our identities. That is, we have a desire not only to express ourselves and our needs to the world, but also to be known, and even ultimately to know ourselves. We can't, and shouldn't, avoid asking and answering the question of identity. What we need are better answers.

The seeds for this book were planted in a time of great personal transition; *crisis* is perhaps not too strong a word. For five years, I was a seminarian studying to become a Catholic priest. In the final months leading up to my diaconate ordination, I couldn't shake the sense that I was making a mistake and that the priesthood wasn't where God wanted me. Eventually, I trusted that my unsettledness wasn't a temptation or my selfishness or last-minute anxiety, but something coming from God — an invitation to step out into the unknown. What I hadn't expected was how profoundly it would impact my sense of identity. For the prior half decade, if anyone asked me who I was, my stock answer was "I'm Joe Heschmeyer. I'm a seminarian for the Archdiocese of Kansas City in Kansas." Suddenly, the last eleven of those fourteen words weren't true.

During this transitional period, I was engaged in college ministry alongside some youth ministers and FOCUS missionaries. Like many missionaries, they had begun their mission with a great deal of idealism, grand visions of leading souls to Christ. Now, a few months into the endeavor, they were feeling discouraged by the lack of results and even a lack of student interest. Each of us was asking, in our own way, "God, I'm trying to do this thing for you: Why isn't it going well?" I asked permission to lead the next week's Bible study, and my original plan was to base it on the themes of success and failure. But the more I delved into the topic, the more I realized that we really needed to talk about identity: that Christ was calling us to something even deeper than missionary or seminarian, and that success or failure would flow from our realization of that deeper identity.

"Who Do People Say That I Am?"

Where do we find these better answers? For starters, in Caesarea Philippi, an ancient town on the northern edge of what was, in the first century, part of the territory of King Herod's son Philip the Tetrarch. It's here that Jesus brings his disciples and asks them a life-changing question: "Who do you say that I am?" One of the disciples, Simon, answers correctly: "You are the Christ, the Son of the living God." Jesus then responds:

> Blessed are you, Simon Bar-Jona! For flesh and blood has not revealed this to you, but my Father who is in heaven. And I tell you, you are Peter, and on this rock I will build my church, and the gates of Hades shall not prevail against it. I will give you the keys of the kingdom of heaven, and whatever you bind on earth shall be bound in heaven, and whatever you loose on earth shall be loosed in heaven. (Matthew 16:16–19)

We'll take a closer look at this passage in chapter 7, but there are two important details to recognize right now. First, it is Jesus who reveals to Simon his deepest identity as Saint Peter. But related to this is a second point: Only after Simon declares Jesus to be "the Son of the living God" does Jesus declare Simon to be "the son of Jonah," which is what "Bar-Jona" means. In other words, the question of "Who am I?" can be accurately answered only by first answering "Who is Jesus?"

But asking "Who is Jesus?" is just the first step. Step two is to let Jesus reveal to us who we are. Simon can't figure out who he is or what he's for on his own, and we know all too well that we can't figure out who we are either. God, as the one who designed us, knows why he designed us, and for what purpose. Ultimately, we need to allow ourselves to be transformed. Remember, our actions are rooted in our identities. How we understand ourselves dictates how we act. This means that when Jesus shows us who he made us to be, that new knowledge changes things. It's a matter not of a static identification but of a dynamic invitation to be who we were meant to be, to become who we truly are. Simon was invited to become Peter, the rock. So radically does Simon's life change due to his encounter with the Messiah that he's given a new name; most Christians know that. But did you know that Jesus makes us the same offer in Revelation 2:17? "To him who conquers I will give some of the hidden manna, and I will give him a white stone, with a new name written on the stone which no one knows except him who receives it."

To put it another way, there's a reason Handel's *Messiah* is divided into three parts. Part 1 recalls the Old Testament Messianic prophecies, followed by Christ's conception, birth, and public ministry. Part 2 depicts his Passion, Death, and Resurrection, ending in the famous "Hallelujah" chorus. You might expect the work to end here, but it doesn't. Part 3 is about the Final Judgment, our redemption from sin, and our eternal life. In other words, the Resurrection isn't the end of the story. In an important sense, it's the beginning of the story: "Christ has been raised from the dead, the first fruits of those who have fallen asleep" (1 Cor 15:20). A similar sort of division occurs in this book: The first half is on who Christ is, including the events of his life and his death and resurrection. The second part looks at what that means for us. We will follow Peter's lead and let Christ reveal us to ourselves.

The Gospel is meant to be transformative, and finding our identity in Christ is quite literally empowering. In Simon Peter's case, it meant receiving the keys to the kingdom of heaven and the power to bind and loose sins. Every Christian has been empowered by God, and only once we know Jesus Christ and his promises can we understand "what God has prepared for those who love him" (1 Cor 2:9). That's what this book is all about. The chapters are laid out as follows:

Part I: Who Do You Say That I Am? *The Identity of Christ*	**Part II: Who Does He Say That You Are?** *God's Promises to Us*
Chapter 1: Perfect Image of God "The image of the invisible God, the first-born of all creation" (Col 1:15)	**Chapter 5: Image of God** "So God created man in his own image, in the image of God he created him" (Gn 1:27)
Chapter 2: Son of God "My beloved Son, with whom I am well pleased" (Mt 3:17)	**Chapter 6: Child of God** "Beloved, we are God's children now" (1 Jn 3:2)
Chapter 3: The Name above All Names "Above every name that is named, not only in this age but also in that which is to come" (Eph 1:21)	**Chapter 7: Your New Name** "I will give him a white stone, with a new name written on the stone which no one knows except him who receives it." (Rv 2:17)
Chapter 4: Lord and God "My Lord and my God!" (Jn 20:28)	**Chapter 8: Partaker of the Divine Nature** "Become partakers of the divine nature" (2 Pt 1:4)

The structure is modeled on what is called a "diptych" in the art world: a set of two panels, connected by a hinge, that has been used throughout the history of Christian art to depict one of the faith's many paradoxes. "Christ is both fully human and fully divine, both dead and alive — and the diptych offered reconciliation" by setting two events alongside one another, inviting the viewer to consider the connections (and the important similarities and dissimilarities) between the two.[30]

Consider, for example, the fifteenth-century *Crucifixion and Last Judgment* diptych depicted here (to help your visualization, you may view the color version available on the website of the Metropolitan Museum of Art), likely painted by Jan van Eyck (1390–1441) or his brother Hubert.[31] The juxtaposition of the two scenes is intended to stir up a sense of contemplation. On the left, we see the soldiers, the crowds, and the chief priests as they mock and laugh and sneer at Christ. The holy women, meanwhile, appear inconsolable. But Jesus taught, "Blessed are those who mourn, for they shall be comforted" (Mt 5:4), and warned, "Woe to you that laugh now, for you shall mourn and weep" (Lk 6:25). And the right side of the diptych reminds us of this: The grieving saints are in heavenly glory, while the unrepentant wicked are damned.

The crosses themselves, especially Christ's, are the "only obvious deviation from the rules of perspective," in that they soar above the mob below. The whole panel is reminiscent of Christ's description of his Passion: "Now is the judgment of this world, now shall the ruler of this world be cast out; and I, when I am lifted up from the earth, will draw all men to myself" (Jn 12:31–32). The crucifixion is the "judgment of the world," both in the sense that the worldly powers judged Christ and condemned him to death, and in the sense that the world itself was thereby judged and found wanting. Fittingly, one of the elements in common between the two panels is that Christ is depicted with the cross in each: the second time, it's more visibly his throne in heavenly glory.

These two paragraphs merely scratch the surface of the painting's complexity, but that's the point. The task of both the painter and the viewer is to draw out the connections between the two panels. How does what's presented on one panel relate to what's presented on the other? I invite you to hold that question in mind as you read this book. In part 1, we'll look at the identity of Christ, because it's only when we recognize who he is that he can show us who we are, as we saw in the story of Peter. Part 2 explores our identity in Christ, in light of four promises God makes to us: that we are made in the image of God, that we have become children of God, that we are promised new names, and that we are destined for divinization.

Finally, I encourage you to read this book in a spirit of prayer. Such an attitude is crucial if you are to glean whatever God wants for you from this book and to grow in your understanding of Jesus, of yourself, and of your neighbor. After all, Simon is able to identify Christ only because he has received that inspiration from the Father, as Jesus says: "Flesh and blood has not revealed this to you, but my Father who is in heaven" (Mt 16:17). In one of the meditations in his famous *Introduction to the Devout Life*, Saint Francis de Sales encourages his readers to pray with Saint Augustine's humble request "O Lord, make me to know Thee and to know myself" and Saint Francis of Assisi's question "Lord, who art Thou, and who am I?"[32] We would do well to do the same.

Who Do You Say That I Am?

The Identity of Christ

CHAPTER 1

Jesus, the Image of God

"Bthe apostles at Caesarea Philippi is an odd one. To those of us used to Christianity, it may seem like a familiar question, but compare Christ with Moses or even with Muhammad, and you can see how odd it is. God said to Moses, "See, I make you as God to Pharaoh; and Aaron your brother shall be your prophet. You shall speak all that I command you; and Aaron your brother shall tell Pharaoh to let the people of Israel go out of his land" (Ex 7:1–2). Likewise, Allah is depicted in the Quran as saying, "Indeed, We have sent to you a messenger as a witness over you, just as We sent a messenger to Pharaoh" (Quran 73:15); "Obey Allah and obey the Messenger! But if you turn away, then Our Messenger's duty is only to deliver 'the message' clearly" (64:12).[1] In each case, the roles are easily understood both by the men themselves and by those to whom they preach. Moses, Aaron, and Muhammad are depicted as mere messengers. There's never any question of their asking others, "Who do you say that I am?" because it wasn't supposed to be about them in the first place.

In comparison, Jesus' question is startling. As Bishop Robert Barron observes, "He doesn't ask what people are saying about his preaching or his miracle-working or his impact on the culture; he asks who they say he *is*."[2] Stranger still, the question seems to leave the apostles dumbfounded, at least initially: Although Jesus asks this question of all of the Twelve, only one of them replies (see Mt 16:15–16). Barron comments, "It is most instructive that silence ensued. Not even the intimate company of the Lord knew the answer."[3]

Is Jesus simply a prophetic messenger, like Moses? Even the crowds seem to think he's more than this. Before asking the apostles their thoughts, Jesus asked them about popular opinion: "Who do men say that the Son of man is?" (Mt 16:13). Mark and Luke's parallel accounts make it clearer that Jesus is asking about himself: "Who do the people say that I am?" (see Mk 8:27; Lk 9:18). The apostles respond, "Some say John the Baptist, others say Elijah, and others Jeremiah or one of the prophets" (Mt 16:13–14). On one level, this is straightforward: Each of the candidates named is a prophet. But what is bizarre is that each of these prophets is dead. In the face of Jesus' miraculous power, even King Herod speculates: "This is John the Baptist; he has been raised from the dead; that is why these powers are at work in him" (Mt 14:2). Something is strange about Jesus, leading even sober-minded people to wonder if he has come from the Great Beyond.

In a very real sense, we can say that the entire New Testament is devoted to unpacking this mystery of who Jesus is. One of the clearest answers comes at the beginning of the Epistle to the Hebrews, as Saint Paul situates Jesus in relation to the Old Testament prophets:

> In many and various ways God spoke of old to our fathers by the prophets; but in these last days he has spoken to us by a Son, whom he appointed the heir of all things, through whom also he created the ages. He reflects the glory of God and bears the very stamp of his nature, upholding the universe by his word of power. When he had made purification for sins, he sat down at the right hand of the Majesty on high, having become as

much superior to angels as the name he has obtained is
more excellent than theirs. (1:1–4)

Within the span of four verses, the epistle highlights four dimensions of the identity of Christ: (1) He is the fullness of prophetic revelation, the full Word of God spoken by the Father;
(2) He is the Son of God; (3) He has a name above that of the
angels; and (4) He is Lord and God. This last identity is only
hinted at, describing Christ as bearing "the very stamp" of the
divine nature, but the text is clear that Jesus is responsible both
for creating the entire universe and for sustaining it in existence
at every moment.

Hebrews is not alone in describing Jesus in this way. We find
a similar description in Colossians 1:15–20:

> He is the image of the invisible God, the first-born of all
> creation; for in him all things were created, in heaven
> and on earth, visible and invisible, whether thrones or
> dominions or principalities or authorities — all things
> were created through him and for him. He is before all
> things, and in him all things hold together. He is the
> head of the body, the Church; he is the beginning, the
> first-born from the dead, that in everything he might
> be pre-eminent. For in him all the fulness of God was
> pleased to dwell, and through him to reconcile to him-
> self all things, whether on earth or in heaven, making
> peace by the blood of his cross.

This chapter and the next three are dedicated to unpacking
each of these four aspects of Christ's identity: Image, Son, Name
above All Names, and Lord and God. We'll begin with the no-
tion of Christ as the full revelation of God. What does Saint Paul
mean by calling Christ the "image of the invisible God"? What's
the relationship of this title to Hebrews' description of Christ as
the complete revelation spoken by the Father?

A God Beyond All Praising

When Saint Paul speaks of the "invisible God," he's referring to a God invisible even to our mind's eye. The first and most radical thing that must be understood about God is that he is, as Saint Anselm of Canterbury (1033–1109) put it, "that than which a greater cannot be thought."[4] At first, this description seems needlessly cumbersome, and many philosophy texts on Anselmic theology "simplify" this as "the greatest being imaginable."[5] That's a huge mistake, because there's a reason Anselm chose the wording he did: The greatest thing you can imagine *is still infinitely short of God.*

This isn't a tiny dispute over wording if we want to understand who and what God is. To understand the theological problem, consider what has been called the "catch-22 of the biology of consciousness."[6] Consider all of the attempts to understand the human brain and the human mind by neurologists, biologists, psychologists, psychiatrists, criminologists, sociologists, anthropologists, and a litany of other scientists and professionals. Each captures something of the truth, yet none of these endeavors has achieved any great success in understanding the inner workings of the human brain, or of the mind, or of predicting human behavior. Some thinkers naïvely imagine that we're on the cusp of overcoming this problem, but anyone closely acquainted with the field can tell you that's just not so. It's not that our science or technology isn't sophisticated enough. As the physicist Emerson M. Pugh neatly put it: "If the human brain were so simple that we could understand it, we would be so simple that we couldn't."[7]

No matter how much technology we design, we'll never be smart enough or informed enough to comprehend our brains fully. And if we can understand our brains only a little, how much can we realistically expect to understand God? He is the Creator not only of our brains and our minds but of the entire cosmos, from the smallest quark to the largest supercluster of galaxies — and these are just his works. God himself is infinitely greater than even the sum of his creation. That's why there's such an enormous chasm (literally, an infinite one) between God as "the greatest being imaginable" and God as "that than which a greater cannot be thought." Perhaps this second phrase, the true one, strikes us as confusing. Good! It ought to.

One of the implications of God's infinity is that every way we try to understand or depict God falls short. How can such a God be known? There's an important difference between knowing God and knowing about God, but let's start with the latter. The short answer is that God can't be comprehended (known completely), but he can be known somewhat. Even the person who claims "God is inherently unknowable" is claiming to know something about God. So how do we know anything about God? By observing his effects, which are all of creation. As Saint Thomas Aquinas (1225–1274) explains, because "human knowledge takes its rise from sense, we can know sufficiently those things that present themselves to our senses. But we can arrive at a knowledge of higher things from them only by way of those things that they have in common with the sensible things that we know."[8]

To get a sense for what Aquinas means, consider the way that crime-scene investigators solve crimes that they didn't witness. They can take a clue, say, footprints left at the scene, and draw conclusions about the one who left the prints. Some questions would be obvious: Were these prints left by an adult or a child, by a human or an animal? But trained experts can sometimes tell a great deal more: whether the person was flat-footed, how worn the shoes were, whether the person was walking or running away, and even the person's approximate height.[9] At the very least, even an amateur could say, "Whoever left these had feet big enough to leave prints this size!" Something like this is what Aquinas means when he says that the cause "is in the effect in the mode belonging to the effect."[10] The Maker of the universe is the kind of Creator capable of making a universe with this much beauty, order, and grandeur. Welcome to *CSI: Theology*.

As Saint Paul points out, evidence of God is available for

everyone. Whether or not you've read the Bible, or even heard of Jesus Christ, you've certainly encountered creation. It's all around you, and it includes you. And so Paul rebukes those who "by their wickedness suppress the truth," since "what can be known about God is plain to them, because God has shown it to them. Ever since the creation of the world his invisible nature, namely, his eternal power and deity, has been clearly perceived in the things that have been made" (Rom 1:18–20). Paul criticizes idolaters for exchanging "the glory of the immortal God for images resembling mortal man or birds or animals or reptiles" (Rom 1:23). *CSI: Theology* is all you need to see the absurdity of idolatry. God is certainly not a creature from within the universe, just as the footprints at the crime scene weren't left by one of the tracks themselves. In either case, the conclusion is patently false, because the effect would be greater than the cause.

Paul's rebuke of idolaters points us to one of life's many paradoxes. We know everything through our senses, and yet we know that this whole sensible world is created and that this can't be all that there is. Everything we encounter daily is contingent, meaning that it didn't have to be here. You wouldn't be here if your parents had never met; the trees wouldn't be here if they hadn't been planted; and so on. This is true of literally everything that we see, hear, taste, smell, and touch every day. And yet we know logically that contingent things can't be *all* that there is, since contingent things need something else to exist. If you need A in order to have B, and you need B in order to have A, you'll never end up with either A or B. There logically *must* be something noncontingent, something necessary. This something (or Someone) is by definition uncreated, since created things are contingent. And so our minds always point beyond the created, contingent realities that we encounter every day, pointing toward the invisible "Uncaused Cause" of it all. So it's easy to see both why idolatry is unreasonable and why it has proven to be so attractive. People want what they're used to, and it's hard to take the mental step from visible created realities to their invisible Creator. Those of us in the First

World are less likely to offer up animal sacrifices to idols these days, but we still largely fall prey to the same mistake that the idolaters did. For instance, we encounter this same inability to see past material things in objections such as "But who caused God?" as if God were yet another part of creation. We see this limitation also in our obsession with, and constant prioritization of, fleeting material things over eternal invisible things. Work is treated as more important than worship because worship has no tangible, visible results. And this is what we regularly call "the real world," with no sense of irony.[11]

Every human being is called to see past the material world, or rather, to see through it. You can know a fair bit about the mind of Shakespeare simply by reading his works. Conversely, knowing a bit about the author can shed light on the meaning of particular parts of his work. But both conclusions require you to realize that the Shakespearean corpus must have had an author. Someone who rejected the very idea of an author and treated the books as having materialized out of spilt ink would be in a very bad position to interpret their meaning. If the books were just the product of a bizarre ink spill, they would *have* no meaning. We must encounter the world through our senses, but we must use this sensory information as "stepping stones," or even as icons that point past themselves toward God. We can learn about God from creation, provided we take that next step. Our rational ability to see through creation to the Creator is our only way of either knowing anything about God or uncovering the meaning of life.

The Ultimate Image of God

While we are called to see through the material world, we repeatedly fall into the trap of idolatry instead. An incomprehensible, infinite, invisible God seems to be almost too much for our minds to grasp or our hearts to accept. But let's consider two scientific facts. The first is that we're hardwired for God. Harvard psychologist Steven Pinker calls "the universal propensity toward religious belief" a "genuine scientific puzzle," but make no mistake:

> There certainly is a phenomenon that needs to be explained, namely, religious beliefs. According to surveys by ethnographers, religion is a human universal. In all human cultures, people believe that the soul lives on after death, that ritual can change the physical world and divine the truth, and that illness and misfortune are caused and alleviated by a variety of invisible personlike entities: spirits, ghosts, saints, evils, demons, cherubim or Jesus, devils, and gods. All cultures? you might ask. Yes, all cultures.[12]

Religion can't be explained away as a merely cultural phenomenon, both because we find it across unconnected cultures throughout the millennia and because we find it surviving and flourishing even in the face of bloody persecution by the state. Something within human beings leads them toward belief in God. And this conclusion isn't coming from a fan of religion, either. Pinker rejects the idea that religion is an evolutionary adaptation, because "the only way religious belief could be an adaptation is if a personal, intervening, miracle-producing, reward-giving, retributive god exists."[13] Since he can't possibly accept that conclusion, he's left with a "genuine scientific puzzle" as to how to explain this universal desire for God.[14]

But we're also hardwired for human connection. A part of the brain, called the fusiform face area (FFA), is dedicated to the recognition of faces.[15] Susan Pinker (a psychologist and, coincidentally, the sister of Steven Pinker), summarizing the emerging evidence "from the fields of social neuroscience and epidemiology," concludes that "daily face-to-face contact with a tight group of friends and family helps you live longer — by fortifying your immune system, calibrating your hormones, and rejigging how the genes that govern your behavior and resilience are expressed."[16] Everything from road rage to Internet trolling to depression can be linked to a failure to get sufficient face-to-face interaction. Sometimes, in a phenomenon called pareidolia, observed in infants as young as eight months old, humans see faces where there are none: in the clouds, on the surface of the moon, in a piece of burnt toast.[17] We crave, and need, face-to-face connection.

Understood in this way, idolatry is our need for a face-to-face connection combined with our desire for God. No wonder, then, that the psalmist says "My heart says to you, 'Your face, LORD, do I seek'" (Ps 27:8). Faced with a faceless God, many of our ancestors opted instead for the faces of "images resembling mortal man or birds or animals or reptiles" (Rom 1:23).

And how does God respond to this human conundrum? As Saint Athanasius of Alexandria (A.D. 296–373) describes, when "the minds of men had fallen finally to the level of sensible things, the Word submitted to appear in a body, in order that he, as Man, might center their senses on himself, and convince them through his human acts that he himself is not man only but also God, the Word and Wisdom of the true God."[18] Jesus Christ, the invisible and eternal God of the universe, enters the world as a baby. Suddenly, God has a face. In the words of Pope Francis, "Jesus Christ is the face of the Father's mercy. These words might well sum up the mystery of the Christian faith."[19] It's as if, after his people had fallen into the worship of images for eons, God responded by mercifully giving them an image they *could* worship: his Son, appearing in the flesh. This, at long last, proved to be a cure for idolatry: "When did people begin to abandon the worship of idols, unless it were since the very Word of God came among men?"[20]

At the heart of the mystery of the Incarnation is the fact that Jesus doesn't cease to be the invisible, almighty God. One of the early Roman apologists against Christianity misunderstood the religion as teaching that the Son of God ceased to reign omnipotently in heaven by becoming a child in Bethlehem. Not so.

Christ became a man without any reduction in his divinity. The shepherds didn't see Christ in his eternity and infinitude and omnipotence, but they did see the eternal, infinite, almighty God in the manger. Christ's visible actions point to his invisible nature: just as God is invisible in himself, but known from the works of creation, "so also, when his Godhead is veiled in human nature, his bodily acts still declare Him to be not man only, but the Power and Word of God."[21]

But in calling him the "image of God," aren't we suggesting that Jesus is less than God? Saint John Damascene (A.D. 676–749) points out that "an image is a likeness of the original *with a certain difference*, for it is not an exact reproduction of the original."[22] Doesn't that mean that Jesus is almost God, an imperfect replica? No. Jesus is the image of the Father. He resembles the Father, sharing one being with him, but is a different Divine Person. John explains that "the Son is the living, substantial, unchangeable Image of the invisible God," since he bears "in Himself the whole Father, being in all things equal to Him, differing only in being begotten by the Father, who is the Begetter; the Son is begotten. The Father does not proceed from the Son, but the Son from the Father. It is through the Son, though not after Him, that He is what He is, the Father who generates."[23]

Christ "reflects the glory of God and bears the very stamp of his nature" (Heb 1:3). Saint Paul speaks of Christ being "the likeness of God," for "it is the God who said, 'Let light shine out of darkness,' who has shone in our hearts to give the light of the knowledge of the glory of God in the face of Christ" (2 Cor 4:6). In referring to "God" here, Paul has in mind God the Father in particular: "the God of our Lord Jesus Christ, the Father of glory" (Eph 1:17). All of this appears to be what Christ reveals to the apostles at the Last Supper when he says, "I am the way, and the truth, and the life; no one comes to the Father, but by me. If you had known me, you would have known my Father also; henceforth you know him and have seen him." After Philip responds "Lord, show us the Father, and we shall be satisfied,"

Jesus reiterates,

> Have I been with you so long, and yet you do not know
> me, Philip? He who has seen me has seen the Father;
> how can you say, "Show us the Father"? Do you not be-
> lieve that I am in the Father and the Father is in me? The
> words that I say to you I do not speak on my own au-
> thority; but the Father who dwells in me does his works.
> Believe me that I am in the Father and the Father in me;
> or else believe me for the sake of the works themselves.
> (John 14:6–11)

From this, we can see that packed into the concept of the "image
of God" is both similarity and difference. Jesus isn't the Father,
but because he (a) shares a common divine nature with the Father and (b) has the Father dwelling within him, we can know
what God the Father is like by looking at God the Son. But is the
idea of Christ as the image of God compatible with his also being
God? To answer this, let us explore a related angle: Christ as the
full revelation of God.

The Full Revelation of God

In calling Christ the "image of the invisible God," Saint Paul
is speaking of him as the revelation of God. "He who has seen
me has seen the Father." Elsewhere, Christ proclaims, "All things
have been delivered to me by my Father; and no one knows the
Son except the Father, and no one knows the Father except the
Son and any one to whom the Son chooses to reveal him" (Mt
11:27). Christ as the revelation of the Father is closely linked to
the Johannine image of Christ as the Word of God. In Isaiah,
God speaks of his word as proceeding from his mouth, and then
returning to him: "For as the rain and the snow come down from
heaven, and do not return there but water the earth, making it
bring forth and sprout, giving seed to the sower and bread to
the eater, so shall my word be that goes forth from my mouth; it

shall not return to me empty, but it shall accomplish that which I intend, and prosper in the thing for which I sent it" (Is 55:10–11). In the Prologue to his Gospel, John shows us how this is true of Jesus as the eternal, ultimate, incarnate Word of God:

> In the beginning was the Word, and the Word was with God, and the Word was God. He was in the beginning with God; all things were made through him, and without him was not anything made that was made. In him was life, and the life was the light of men. The light shines in the darkness, and the darkness has not overcome it. … And the Word became flesh and dwelt among us, full of grace and truth; we have beheld his glory, glory as of the only-begotten Son from the Father. (John 1:1–5, 14)

How do we harmonize the idea of Jesus as the image, the word, the revelation, and the messenger of God with the idea that Jesus is himself God? Quite simply, what God wishes to reveal in his revelation is *himself.* So the only way to reveal God fully is through God. Were Jesus less than divine, he would be less than the full revelation of God. A nondivine person could be a messenger, but not the message; a revelator, but not the revelation. Christ is the fullness of the revelation of God precisely because he is both the eternal God and a visible man. "No one has ever seen God; the only-begotten Son, who is in the bosom of the Father, he has made him known" (Jn 1:18). That's what it means to say that Christ is the "image of the invisible God." He is the fullness of the revelation of God.

This means that Christianity, properly understood, is not a "religion of the system," or even a "religion of the book," but a "religion of the Word" — that is, a religion of Jesus the Word (see the *Catechism of the Catholic Church* [CCC] 108). Saint Bernard of Clairvaux (1090–1153) puts beautifully what it means for the religion to be "of the Word":

May He be to me not only audible to my ears, but visible to my eyes, felt by my hands, borne in my arms. Let Him be to me not a mute and written word traced with dumb signs on lifeless parchments, but an Incarnate, living Word vividly impressed in human form in my chaste womb by the operation of the Holy Ghost.[24]

How does this contrast with reductions of Christianity to a "religion of the system" or a "religion of the book"?

A Religion of the System?

In the first category are those who want to accept Jesus' teaching (or parts of it) and his "way of life," without accepting his claimed divinity. Frequently, it is an attempt to separate the morality of Christianity from the religion of Christianity. For example, the author Kurt Vonnegut explained his religious approach this way:

I am a humanist, which means, in part, that I have tried to behave decently without any expectation of rewards or punishments after I'm dead. My German-American ancestors, the earliest of whom settled in our Middle West about the time of our Civil War, called themselves "Freethinkers," which is the same sort of thing. My great grandfather Clemens Vonnegut wrote, for example, "If what Jesus said was good, what can it matter whether he was God or not?"

I myself have written, "If it weren't for the message of mercy and pity in Jesus' Sermon on the Mount, I wouldn't want to be a human being. I would just as soon be a rattlesnake."[25]

The simplest answer to Clemens Vonnegut's question is that, if Jesus wasn't God, then what he said wasn't good. Jesus expresses the stakes quite clearly:

> Do not think that I have come to bring peace on earth;
> I have not come to bring peace, but a sword. For I have
> come to set a man against his father, and a daughter
> against her mother, and a daughter-in-law against her
> mother-in-law; and a man's foes will be those of his own
> household. He who loves father or mother more than
> me is not worthy of me; and he who loves son or daugh-
> ter more than me is not worthy of me; and he who does
> not take his cross and follow me is not worthy of me. He
> who finds his life will lose it, and he who loses his life for
> my sake will find it. (Matthew 10:34–39)

Jesus established Christianity, making no apologies for the fact
that it would be divisive, even separating families. If Jesus wasn't
God, then what he said was divisive blasphemy that got a lot of
people killed — and sent to hell — for no good reason. Jesus
could hardly have been surprised that the new religion would
be viewed as blasphemy by many Jews and as dangerous subver-
sion by the Romans. And the whole reason Christianity was so
controversial in a Jewish context is that blasphemy is damnable;
so followers of a false religion would have only worse things to
look forward to after death. Saint Paul points all of this out to
the Corinthians:

> If Christ has not been raised, then our preaching is in
> vain and your faith is in vain. We are even found to be
> misrepresenting God, because we testified of God that
> he raised Christ, whom he did not raise if it is true that
> the dead are not raised. For if the dead are not raised,
> then Christ has not been raised. If Christ has not been
> raised, your faith is futile and you are still in your sins.
> Then those also who have fallen asleep in Christ have
> perished. If for this life only we have hoped in Christ, we
> are of all men most to be pitied. (1 Corinthians 15:14–19)

Even the Sermon on the Mount ends with Jesus saying, "Blessed are you when men revile you and persecute you and utter all kinds of evil against you falsely on my account. Rejoice and be glad, for your reward is great in heaven, for so men persecuted the prophets who were before you" (Mt 5:11–12). This promise is good only if it's true, and it's true only if Jesus Christ really is who he says he is.

Within the Christian framework, Jesus isn't just the messenger; he's also the message. This is why it doesn't work to claim to accept "the message of Jesus" while rejecting or sidestepping his divine claim. You can understand Judaism without knowing much of anything about the prophets — it's their message, rather than their biography, that mostly concerns us. So, too, there's relatively little to be learned about Joseph Smith or Muhammad from the Book of Mormon or the Quran. Each of those authors understood themselves as messengers, delivering a message more important than themselves or their own lives. But you can't understand the Christian Gospel without understanding the person of Jesus Christ, which is why he asks the odd question "Who do you say that I am?" If you don't understand him, you don't understand the message of Christianity.

A Religion of the Book?

Another common misunderstanding of Christianity is that it's a "religion of the book." This claim is found explicitly in the Quran, which refers to Christians and Jews as "People of the Book" (5:15). Allah is depicted as saying that "in the footsteps of the prophets, We sent Jesus, son of Mary, confirming the Torah revealed before him. And We gave him the Gospel containing guidance and light and confirming what was revealed in the Torah — a guide and a lesson to the God-fearing" (5:46). The idea is that God gave the Jews the Torah, Christians "the Gospel" (meaning the New Testament), and Muslims the Quran.

But that's not at all how Jesus is presented in the Gospels. He didn't come to deliver a book, and he didn't write a word of Scripture during his lifetime. This means that a good deal of Christian infighting over whether the fullness of revelation is "Scripture alone" or "Scripture and Tradition" is completely off base. The fullness of revelation is Jesus Christ. Christ did not come to bring us "the Gospel" in the sense of the New Testament. Instead, the New Testament presents the Gospel, the Good News that is Jesus Christ. Scripture exists to bring us to Jesus, not the other way around. Indeed, Jesus critiques those who ignore him while focusing on Scripture:

> And the Father who sent me has himself borne witness to me. His voice you have never heard, his form you have never seen; and you do not have his word abiding in you, for you do not believe him whom he has sent. You search the Scriptures, because you think that in them you have eternal life; and it is they that bear witness to me; yet you refuse to come to me that you may have life. (John 5:37–40)

If you want to see the tension between a "religion of the book" and a "religion of the Word," look at how we understand Hebrews 4:12–13, which says that the Word of God, the Logos (λόγος), "is living and active, sharper than any two-edged sword, piercing to the division of soul and spirit, of joints and marrow, and discerning the thoughts and intentions of the heart. And before him no creature is hidden, but all are open and laid bare to the eyes of him with whom we have to do." For early Christians, the *Logos* of Hebrews 4:12–13 was understood to be the same *Logos* of John 1: namely, Jesus Christ. Today, though, many Christians assume that "the word of God" refers to the Bible.[26]

Dr. Telford Work, a theologian at Westmont College, in a work aptly titled *Living and Active: Scripture in the Economy of Salvation*, claims that "the Word of God" in places such as Hebrews 4:12 refers to "the word orally proclaimed in a particular setting by a prophet or apostle."[27] He seems confused to find

Church Fathers such as Saint Athanasius applying Hebrews 4:12 to Jesus, and he assumes that the saint is applying it metaphorically: "Remarkably, Athanasius even *transposes* Scripture and Jesus in citing Hebrews 4:12, to affirm that 'the Son of God is "living and active," and works day by day, to bring about the salvation of all' (§ 31)."[28] Work believes that even John's mentions of Jesus as the *Logos* mean that "Jesus is the 'word' in the metaphorical sense that he is the 'uttered' manifestation of God's grace and truth."[29] All of this assumes that the full word of God is Scripture, and Jesus is only the Word of God analogously. In contrast, the Epistle to the Hebrews opens by saying that "in many and various ways God spoke of old to our fathers by the prophets; but in these last days he has spoken to us by a Son" (1:1–2), suggesting that God's partial revelation was through the Scriptures (and the various other ways he spoke to us through the prophets), and that his full revelation is his Son.

What It Means to Be a Religion of the Word

Having seen that Christianity isn't a religion of the system, or of the book, what does it mean to say that Christianity is a religion of the Word? It means, in the words of Pope Benedict XVI, that "being Christian is not the result of an ethical choice or a lofty idea, but the encounter with an event, a person, which gives life a new horizon and a decisive direction."[30] It means that a yes to Christianity is less like the intellectual assent we pay to a mathematical equation and more like the acceptance of a suitor's proposal.

Does that mean that Christianity is all about relationship, and not religion? That's a popular idea right now.[31] The "relationship, not religion" cliché has become a byword in some parts of Christianity while "the word *religion* has become a pejorative in the pulpits of too many preachers, and it has spread to the pews, as well."[32] A great example of this trend is Jefferson Bethke's 2010 YouTube video called "Why I Hate Religion, but Love Jesus." Within three days, it had gone viral, receiving more than six million views.[33] Bethke begins by asking, "What if I told you Jesus came to abolish religion?" He goes on to claim that "religion puts you in bondage, while Jesus sets you free" and asserts, "So for religion — no, I hate it; in fact I literally resent it."

Did Christ come to abolish religion? Definitely not. His own promise to Peter — "on this rock I will build my church" (Mt 16:18) — seems to point to the creation of a new religion. Saint Paul likewise speaks of the great "mystery of our religion" (1 Tm 3:16), and Saint James says that "religion that is pure and undefiled before God and the Father is this: to visit orphans and widows in their affliction, and to keep oneself unstained from the world" (Jas 1:27). Is a "relationship" sufficient? Also no. To some of those who will say, "We ate and drank in your presence, and you taught in our streets," he will say, "I tell you, I do not know where you come from; depart from me, all you workers of iniquity!" (Lk 13:26–27). The key is being in *right* relationship with him. If we believe that Jesus is the revelation of God, we cannot separate the messenger from the message. We cannot take his teachings on love and mercy while rejecting his claim to divinity, nor can we accept his claim to be God while ignoring his moral teachings.

And this means also that the Church plays a crucial role, not as an intermediary to get to Christ, or as an obstacle standing in the way of our relationship with Christ, but as a living manifestation of that relationship. To grasp this, we must confront one of the most common mistakes Christians make — treating Jesus as dead and gone. In Tolstoy's novella *The Death of Ivan Ilyich*, a dying man realizes that he has spent his entire life pursuing worldly success and respectability, and that the meaninglessness of this way of living is causing his fear of death. "What if my whole life has been wrong?" he finally asks himself, leading him to see the difference between a lifestyle built on the avoidance of death and a life spent preparing for eternity.[34] Andrew Starks's reading of the novella is that "Ivan himself dies. But because he has been a proficient death denier his life continues on, showing him to have become superfluous to it."[35] What Starks means by saying that Ivan's life "continues on" is that there are always others who are there "to take up Ivan's own role in what would otherwise have been his own life."[36] But this is true precisely because Ivan hasn't lived on, at least in this worldly sense. As the novella title reminds us, Ivan Ilyich is dead.

Each of us can fall into that kind of loose talk. When a loved one dies, instead of focusing on the continued existence of that person's soul as he or she stands in judgment before Almighty God, we'll speak vaguely of how the person's life continues on in his or her loved ones. Of course, we don't really mean that, or we wouldn't be having a funeral. And we do this kind of thing even with Jesus. The temptation in Christianity is to reduce the Resurrection and eternal life of Jesus Christ to a sort of symbol, a mere metaphor of the triumph of good over evil, and to fail to take seriously that he is still alive on earth. We either want to put him back in the grave or to lock him safely away in heaven, while we take care of the Christianity business without him, continuing his legacy in his absence. This is not a new temptation. When Jesus warned them not to tell anyone about the Transfiguration "until the Son of man should have risen from the dead," Peter, James, and John "kept the matter to themselves, questioning what the rising from the dead meant" (Mk 9:9–10). It wasn't until they lived through it that they realized that this was no metaphor or figure of speech. Even today, we find would-be followers of Christ who want to reduce his death and resurrection to a mere symbol. Serene Jones, president of Union Theological Seminary, claimed that people claiming to know that Jesus rose from the dead are "kidding themselves" and that they have a "wobbly faith," since it relies on the literal truth of the Resurrection.[37]

Most of us don't go quite that far. We'll happily affirm the literal Resurrection on Easter Sunday, but then we'll sort of wave goodbye to Jesus forty days later at his Ascension. To be sure, there is a sense in which Jesus' entry into heaven means he's not with us, at least not in precisely the same way that he was before (see Jn 16:7). But it's also true that the last words of the Gospel of Matthew are Jesus' promise: "Behold, I am with you always, to the close of the age" (28:20). Saint Bernard spoke of the present age as a sort of "middle coming" of the Lord, in which Christ continues to be present "in spirit and power." This middle coming is the "road on which we travel from the first coming to the last. In the first, Christ was our redemption; in the last, he will appear as our life; in this middle coming, he is our rest and consolation."[38]

Because this "middle coming" of Christ differs from the other two in that he is not visibly present, we quickly forget his presence, just as the Israelites of old struggled to believe in the presence of a God they couldn't see.[39] And so we talk about what Jesus would think of the Church if he were around to see it today, oblivious to the obvious reality that he does see it today, and that the Church is, in some mysterious way, a continuation of the Incarnation. Saint Paul speaks of the Church as the "Body of Christ" (see Rom 12:5; 1 Cor 12:12–27). It's tempting to take this as a loose metaphor, to mean simply that there's a vague collection of people who are enthusiastic for Jesus, or that he lives on in the Church somewhat as Ivan Ilyich "lives on" in those around him, even though Ivan is literally dead. But Paul doesn't leave us room for that, just as he doesn't leave room for a nonliteral resurrection (see 1 Cor 15:14–20). Instead, he speaks of Jesus, plus the Church, equalling the "fullness" of Christ, saying that God "has put all things under [Christ's] feet and has made him the head over all things for the church, which is his body, the fulness of him who fills all in all" (Eph 1:22–23).

Christianity is about relationship, both with God and with neighbor. But one of the reasons this relationship is possible is that Christ hasn't left us with a message, or a system, or a book. *He* is the message, he is the image of the invisible God, and he continues to be present through his Church and in our souls. One consequence of this is that we cannot fully understand either ourselves or Christianity without first knowing Christ. But if Christ is the ultimate message of Christianity, just who is he? He's clearly a teacher of some kind, but what do we make of his curious teachings, including his claim to be the "Son of God"?

CHAPTER 2
Jesus, the Son of God

"You are my beloved Son; with you I am well pleased" (Lk 3:22). Beginnings matter. Ann Hornaday, chief film critic for the *Washington Post*, explains that "Within the first ten minutes, a well-written movie will teach the audience how to watch it."[1] Books work in largely the same way. The novelist N. M. Kelby advises aspiring authors, "Always begin with your protagonist," since "readers need to discover who the hero is and why they should root for him. Introduce your protagonist, either directly or indirectly, within the first 300 words."[2] Contrast these "best practices" with how the Gospel of Matthew (and thus, the entire New Testament) opens. As Joseph F. Kelly explains, "Matthew's Infancy Narrative appears in chapters 1 and 2 of the gospel. When we turn to his account of Jesus' birth, we find, to our disappointment, that it begins with a boring genealogy of 'so-and-so begat so-and-so' from Abraham, the father of the Jewish people, down to Jesus, the Messiah."[3] In fact, Matthew introduces his Gospel as "the book of the genealogy of Jesus Christ, the son of David, the son of Abraham" (1:1). But at least Matthew gets the genealogies out of the way in the very beginning. After seventeen verses, he transitions by saying, "Now the birth of Jesus Christ took place in this way" (1:18). After this, something approaching a straightforward biographical narrative ensues.

In contrast, Luke relays the genealogies of Jesus right in the middle of the action. Luke recounts the circumstances of Jesus' baptism, with the heavens opening, the Holy Spirit descending upon Jesus, and the voice of God coming from heaven (3:21–22). Then he says, "Jesus, when he began his ministry, was about thirty years of age, being the son (as was supposed) of Joseph, the son of Heli, the son of Matthat, the son of Levi, the son of Melchi, the son of Jannai, the son of Joseph" (3:23–24) and proceeds to trace Jesus' genealogy past Abraham, all the way back to Adam. For the reader, the effect can be a bit akin to that of a filmmaker's running the credits in the middle of an action sequence: It seems abrupt and jarring, and we want it to end quickly so that we can get back to the action. When Luke finally finishes, he picks up right where he left off: "And Jesus, full of the Holy Spirit, returned from the Jordan, and was led by the Spirit for forty days in the wilderness, tempted by the devil" (4:1–2a). By mentioning the return from the Jordan, Luke connects what's about to happen in the desert (the temptation of Christ) to what has just happened in the Jordan (his baptism).[4]

Why do Matthew and Luke include these genealogies? Why does Luke interrupt the action to relay Jesus' genealogy right after his baptism? And why does Luke connect the baptism in the Jordan and the temptations in the desert, given that he's the one who has deliberately interrupted his own narrative? Unpacking this requires taking a closer look at the two bookends to Luke's genealogy: Jesus' baptism in the Jordan, and his temptation in the desert. Luke relates the first of these succinctly: "Now when all the people were baptized, and when Jesus also had been baptized and was praying, the heaven was opened, and the Holy Spirit descended upon him in bodily form, as a dove, and a voice came from heaven, 'You are my beloved Son; with you I am well pleased'" (3:21–22). This event is one of only a handful of times in the Bible with clear "Trinitarian theophanies," meaning that we see the Father (the voice from heaven), the Son (Jesus), and the Holy Spirit, each present and distinct from one another. This is also the first of only a handful of times in which we hear God the Father speak. And his words deserve our rapt attention: "You are my beloved Son; with you I am well pleased."

This message, the revelation that Jesus is the Son of God, is an important one. And it turns out, we're not the only ones paying close attention. Moving past the genealogies for now, notice how the temptation of Christ begins: "And Jesus, full of the Holy Spirit, returned from the Jordan, and was led by the Spirit for forty days in the wilderness, tempted by the devil. And he ate nothing in those days; and when they were ended, he was hungry. The devil said to him, 'If you are the Son of God, command this stone to become bread'" (4:1–3).

God the Father has just spoken publicly, and his message is that Jesus is the Son of God. This is the framework through which we should understand Christ's temptation in the desert. Satan has recognized a threat, perhaps deducing what we would later come to know: that "the reason the Son of God appeared was to destroy the works of the devil" (1 Jn 3:8). Whatever the case, the devil immediately sets out to test the divine claim. Frank Sheed reasonably speculates, "I think it was of the first urgency for Satan to find out what 'son of God' meant. It had been used in the Old Testament as a name for the Messiah (Ps. 2:7). But did he know what it *meant*?"[5] The Greek word meaning "to tempt" (*peirazein*, πειράζω) sometimes means "to entice people to do wrong" (as we now use it in English), but in Scripture it more frequently means "to test."[6] Satan appears to be both tempting and testing Jesus here. He wants to find out what it means for Jesus to be a Son of God and to discover a way to undermine or destroy that identity.

After Jesus rebuffs the first temptation, the examination continues. The devil takes Jesus to the pinnacle of the temple in Jerusalem, and says, "If you are the Son of God, throw yourself down" (Mt 4:6; Lk 4:9).[7] We find Satan still trying to determine who Jesus is, probing for cracks in the armor, searching for some sign of weakness. Look at how Jesus answers. When Satan tempts Jesus to turn stones into bread, Jesus responds, "It is written, 'Man shall not live by bread alone, but by every word that proceeds from the mouth of God'" (Mt 4:4). He's quoting Deuteronomy 8:4, which says that God "humbled you and let you hunger and fed you with manna, which you did not know, nor did your fathers know; that he might make you know that man does not live by bread alone, but that man lives by everything that proceeds out of the mouth of the LORD."⁸ The second time, he quotes Deuteronomy 6:16, which says, "You shall not put the LORD your God to the test, as you tested him at Massah." And the final time, when the devil tries to entice Christ to worship him, he says, "Begone, Satan! for it is written, 'You shall worship the Lord your God and him only shall you serve'" (Mt 4:10). This third response is from Deuteronomy 6:13. In other words, Christ responds to Satan's testing with succinct citations of Scripture that both rebuff every temptation and reveal very little about himself. The only thing he adds is "Begone, Satan!"

The responses work. The escalating nature of Satan's temptations seem to reflect his inability to gain any sort of foothold. Sheed points out that when we look at the three things dangled before Jesus by the devil, the direction of the temptations is upward — bread, a spectacular display, the kingdoms of this world. But in relation to the person tempted, the whole movement is downward, almost as though Satan rated him lower and lower — first he is asked to work a miracle by his own power, next to count on angels to help him through, last to prostrate himself before the tempter and call him Lord.⁹

Satan, thwarted, seems unimpressed and departs knowing nothing more about Christ than he knew before, other than that this man can quote Scripture. No new light seems to have been shed on that most mysterious of titles, "Son of God."

Luke also recognizes that this title is of great significance, so it makes perfect sense that he should choose to give us Jesus' human genealogy right here in the midst of things. While it's true that we "do not know about these Old Testament genealogies because almost no one reads them, either on one's own or from a pulpit," we shouldn't forget that "the problem lies not with

Matthew but with us. In the ancient Semitic world, you could not really know who people were unless you knew who their ancestors were."[10] And if we're honest, the reason we find biblical genealogies boring is largely because we don't know our Old Testament history well enough. We find our personal genealogies fascinating: Genealogy is the second most popular hobby in the United States after gardening, and genealogical websites are the second most visited category of websites (unfortunately, you can probably guess the first).[11] By tracing his lineage back to Adam, the first man, Luke makes the point that Christ is the Son of Man as well as the Son of God, both fully man and fully divine.

But there's more to it. In tracing his lineage, Luke isn't just saying that Jesus is biologically human, but that he's part of a family, a family not unlike our own. Like many a family tree, Jesus' ancestors are a decidedly mixed bag, containing patriarchs, kings, child killers, and a prostitute or two. We'll talk about one of the nastiest of these, King Ahaz, in the next chapter. But even many of Jesus' greatest ancestors were deeply flawed in obvious ways. Saint Matthew points out that Judah became "the father of Perez and Zerah by Tamar" (1:3), his own daughter-in-law, whom he slept with after mistaking her for a cult prostitute (see Gn 38). King "David was the father of Solomon by the wife of Uriah" (1:6), an act of adultery that the king covered up by having Uriah killed (2 Sm 11).

Son of God and Son of Man

It's an odd reality that the God of the universe has ancestors, but humanly speaking, he does. Indeed, Jesus seems to take some pleasure in pointing this out to the Pharisees. After they acknowledge (rightly) that the Messiah is the Son of David, Jesus quotes to them the opening line of Psalm 110, in which David said, "The Lord said to my Lord: 'Sit at my right hand until I put your enemies under your feet.'" He then poses to them a stumper of a question: "If David thus calls him Lord, how is he his son?" And it's perhaps no surprise that "no one was able to answer him a word, nor from that day did any one dare to ask him any more questions" (Mt 22:41–46). How can the Messiah be both the son of David, many generations in the future, and the already-existing Lord of David? The Pharisees don't know about the Incarnation, and they don't understand that the Messiah is both fully God and fully man, so they're flummoxed.

These two natures of Christ — human and divine — are why we see two genealogies in Luke 3, not just one. The "divine genealogy" is spoken at the baptism: "You are my beloved Son; with you I am well pleased" (v. 22). The Father declares unequivocally that Jesus is his Son. But Luke points out that Jesus is also a Son of Adam, and so we are given that human genealogy. Interestingly, Luke's genealogy goes back to "Adam, the son of God" (3:38). So we're presented with a mystery: What does it mean to be a "son of God"? There's a sense in which all humans are sons and daughters of God, because God makes us in his image, and after his likeness (see Gn 1:26). We'll talk about that in chapter 5. And there's a deeper sense in which we become sons and daughters of God at our baptisms, which we'll discuss in chapter 6.

But while Jesus is the Son of God in each of these ways, God the Father seems to be revealing something more here. If the Father merely meant to say that Jesus is like everyone else in being made in the image of God, such a fact would seem too obvious to warrant a direct revelation from heaven. No, Jesus is also the Son of God in a different way, in a way true only of him. In John 3:16, he's described as the *monogenēs* (μονογενής) of the Father. Scholars debate whether that should be translated as "only begotten" Son of the Father or as "one and only" Son of the Father, but both are true.[12] In one sense, Jesus is the "only" Son of God, because he's the only one who is "begotten, not made," as the Nicene Creed puts it.

What does that distinction mean? Broadly speaking, there are three types of fatherhood: through creation, through adoption, and through begetting. When we talk about our relationship to the Father (as we will in later chapters), we're speaking in terms of our creation and adoption. God creates us, and in that sense he's a "Father" to us. It's in this first sense, for instance, that we speak of Joseph Engelberger as the "Father of Robotics," because he largely invented the field.[13] But of course, there's a stark difference between someone's relationship to his creation and his relationship to his children. This is where the idea of divine adoption comes in: that God treats us as, and even makes us to be, his children in a fuller sense of the term. This adoption carries with it the promise of inheritance, as Saint Paul says: "if children, then heirs, heirs of God and fellow heirs with Christ" (Rom 8:17). We'll look more into the details of that promised inheritance in chapter 8. For now, notice that we are made "fellow heirs with Christ." The implication is that we are made heirs through adoption, but that Christ is the natural heir. That's because those who aren't one's natural children can become one's children through adoption.

A cat named Nimra, while tending to her litter of four kittens in Madaba, Jordan, "adopted a flock of seven baby chicks that were suddenly orphaned in 2007 after their mother died."[14] Nimra served as a mother to these chicks, though she and they were of entirely different natures. Likewise, our adoption by God is a recognition that we are not, by nature, divine. If we were, we wouldn't need to be adopted. So what does this mean for Jesus of Nazareth? An early heresy (fittingly called "Adoptionism") viewed him as an adopted son of the Father, like us.[15] But John's point in calling Jesus the *monogenē* is that his sonship is quite different from ours (the prefix *mono* means "only," as we recognize from terms such as *monotheism*).

Jesus is, so to speak, the "natural" Son of the Father, meaning that he shares in the nature of his Father. That's the meaning of the term *beget*. It's how we speak of natural generation, as when we hear that "David took more wives in Jerusalem, and David begot more sons and daughters" (1 Chr 14:3). The wording is quite clear that David isn't adopting these children; he's procreating them with his many wives. If our relationship to the Father is like the relationship of those chicks to Nimra, Christ's is more like the relationship of one of those kittens to Nimra.

And anyone looking at Nimra's odd family could recognize which members are and which aren't her natural children by the fact that her natural children share the same sort of nature she has. Cats beget cats. Likewise, in calling Jesus the only begotten of the Father, we're declaring him divine, because God begets God. And this is exactly what John wants us to understand about Jesus, as he tells us at the start of his Gospel:

> In the beginning was the Word, and the Word was with God, and the Word was God. He was in the beginning with God; all things were made through him, and without him was not anything made that was made. ... No one has ever seen God; the only [*monogenē*] Son, who is in the bosom of the Father, he has made him known. (John 1:1–2, 18)

So, Jesus is the *monogenē*, the unique and only-begotten Son of the Father, because he is eternally in the bosom of the Father and proceeds forth from him, like a child coming forth from a parent, or a word coming forth from a speaker. It's for this reason that he can be (as we saw in the last chapter) the full revelation of God: because God is revealing *himself.*

John's language is necessarily a bit cryptic, but for a good reason. God doesn't beget in the same way that we do, through sexual intercourse. Brigham Young, Joseph Smith's successor as head of the Church of Jesus Christ of Latter-day Saints, claimed that "the birth of the Saviour was as natural as are the births of our children; it was the result of natural action. He partook of flesh and blood — was begotten of his Father, as we were of our fathers" — in other words, that God the Father physically impregnated Mary by having sex with her. That's a good description of paganism, but a poor understanding of the Virgin Birth.

Zeus is said to have shapeshifted to appear as Apollos in order to seduce a maiden named Callisto, who had "vowed to the goddess the maintenance of perpetual virginity."[16] Afterward, she was turned into a bear and then murdered by Artemis, who is said to have "shot her because she had failed to preserve her virginity."[17] But Mary, quite famously, did remain a virgin.

Moreover, if Jesus were produced through sexual union, he wouldn't have existed until the first century. And yet, as we've just heard from Saint John, he existed from "the beginning" alongside the Father. This is why we speak of Jesus as "eternally begotten of the Father." In addition to being eternally begotten of the Father, Jesus is also conceived by the Virgin Mary through the power of the Holy Spirit. The angel Gabriel tells her, "You will conceive in your womb and bear a son, and you shall call his name Jesus" (Lk 1:31). Some Protestants, afraid of giving too much dignity to the Virgin Mary, go to the opposite extreme and declare her no more than a "vessel" for Jesus. One view of the Incarnation is that God created (from nothing) "an impregnated ovum within her uterus with no contribution from Mary's own genetic heritage at all," with the result that "Mary is simply a vessel in which is implanted an already fertilized ovum — indeed a kind of surrogate mother."[18]

Reducing Mary to a mere vessel ultimately denies Jesus' humanity, the very humanity affirmed through his scriptural genealogy. If Jesus has no human parents, he has no biological ancestors, no human relatives whatsoever. In short, he would be merely a copy of humanity, without actually being human. In such a case, the Virgin Birth would be largely a façade, giving the appearance of biological motherhood where it did not exist. But Gabriel says the opposite: that Mary will conceive a son in her womb. This is the language of begetting. That's not to say that every detail of the mechanism of the miraculous conception is immediately clear to us. The closest anyone (including Mary) gets to an explanation is the angel Gabriel's promise to her: "The Holy Spirit will come upon you, and the power of the Most High will overshadow you; therefore the child to be born will be called holy, the Son of God" (Lk 1:35). But despite the mysterious and miraculous circumstances of his conception in her womb, Jesus is truly the biological son of Mary. He is fully human, because he's the human son of a human mother, just as he is fully divine, because he is the divine Son of a divine Father.

Here we come to a fascinating detail about the way Jesus describes himself, vis-à-vis the way that his followers tend to describe him. In Hebrew, "son of man" was another way of saying "man," as when King David asks God, "What is man that you are mindful of him, and the son of man that you care for him?" (Ps 8:4). The reason is clear: the son of a cat is a kitten, a baby cat. The son of a man is a man. And so "son of Man" is initially a poetic title that simply means "man"; for the same reason, calling Jesus the "Son of God" implies that he is God.

It's unsurprising that when Jesus' followers describe him, they tend to describe him as the "Son of God." It's not particularly interesting to them that Jesus is a human being. What's remarkable is that this human being is also God. But that doesn't seem to be what strikes Jesus. When he speaks of himself, it's the other way around. Some sixty-nine times in the Gospels, he refers to himself as "Son of Man," often in the third person. It's true that this was already a Messianic title — the prophet Daniel speaks of seeing visions of the Son of Man in the night:

> And behold, with the clouds of heaven there came one like a son of man, and he came to the Ancient of Days and was presented before him. And to him was given dominion and glory and kingdom, that all peoples, nations, and languages should serve him; his dominion is an everlasting dominion, which shall not pass away, and his kingdom one that shall not be destroyed. (Daniel 7:13–14)

But it also seems possible that the thing that Jesus was "struck by" was the Incarnation itself — being God from all eternity, he is now also man. Whatever the case, it's important not to push the point too far: The Evangelists affirm that Jesus, in addition to being divine, is also fully human; and Jesus is clear that, in addition to being human, he is also fully divine. Perhaps no single line summarizes this union between Christ as Son of God and Son of Man more clearly than his own words in Mark 8:38, when he warns that "whoever is ashamed of me and of my words in this adulterous and sinful generation, of him will the Son of man also be ashamed, when he comes in the glory of his Father with the holy angels."

The Obedience of the Son

Christ is the Son of God and the Son of Man. But why focus on the "son" part of this at all? Why not simply say that he's fully God and fully man? Because Christ lives out a perfect obedience to the will of the Father. The distinction between the Father and the Son isn't that one is God and the other isn't, but rather, that "the Father loves the Son, and has given all things into his hand" (Jn 3:35). The Father is the Giver, and the Son is the Receiver. As Sheed explains, "the Son receives his existence and his nature — all that he is and all that he has — from the Father, for that is what being a son means. But he receives *all* that the Father is and has in utter equality," so that Jesus is no less God than the Father is.[19] The Fourth Lateran Council says the same thing: "For the Father begetting the Son from eternity imparted to Him His own substance,"[20] and this also seems to be the meaning of Jesus' declaration "I and the Father are one" (Jn 10:30). That statement was so naked a declaration of his divinity that the crowds picked up rocks to stone him for the crime of blasphemy, crying that "you, being a man, make yourself God" (Jn 10:33).

There's something profound about the Trinity being revealed in all of this, as the Fourth Lateran Council rightly recognized. But let's save that discussion for chapter 4. For now, simply recognize the humility and obedience of the Son. Despite being all-powerful, all-knowing, and coequal with the Father, at every turn, he remains entirely dependent on the Father. "Truly, truly, I say to you," Jesus says, "the Son can do nothing of his own accord, but only what he sees the Father doing; for whatever he does, that the Son does likewise" (Jn 5:19). This humility is born not of weakness, but of love. That is, Christ is not denying his omnipotence (that he is all-powerful) but affirming his omnibenevolence (that he is all-good).

The interplay between these two aspects of Jesus' divine Sonship — his absolute power and authority coupled with his complete and total reliance on the Father — allow him to face any obstacle, even the cross, with grace and aplomb. "When you have lifted up the Son of man, then you will know that I am he, and that I do nothing on my own authority but speak thus as the Father taught me. And he who sent me is with me; he has not left me alone, for I always do what is pleasing to him" (Jn 8:28–29). In the same instant, Jesus declares himself YHWH, the "I AM" revealed in the Old Testament (a title we'll explore more in the next two chapters), and presents himself as the perfectly obedient Son of the Father.

CHAPTER 3

Jesus, the Name
Above All Names

"Call me Ishmael. Some years ago — never mind how long precisely — having little or no money in my purse, and nothing particular to interest me on shore, I thought I would sail about a little and see the watery part of the world."[1] So begins Herman Melville's novel *Moby Dick*. We saw in the last chapter that openers matter, and nothing beats this opener. *American Book Review* puts the first three words, "Call me Ishmael," in the number-one spot in its "100 Best First Lines from Novels."[2] Perhaps the only personal introduction that can rival this is in *The Princess Bride*, in which the Spanish swordsman repeatedly introduces himself to his adversary by declaring, "Hello, my name is Inigo Montoya; you killed my father, prepare to die."[3]

In its own way, each work points to the importance of names. Inigo Montoya's declaration of his name is a profound moment of self-assertion and, with the invocation of his family name, a moment of vindication for his father. *Moby Dick*'s ambiguous "Call me Ishmael" leaves us wondering about the narrator's real name and, by extension, questioning his honesty and reliability. Or consider the famous balcony scene from act 2, scene 2 of *Romeo and Juliet*.[4] The scene is chock-full of memorable lines, but perhaps the most famous is Juliet's famous declaration to Romeo: "What's in a name? That which we call a rose by any other

word would smell as sweet." Juliet has learned that Romeo is of
the house of Montague, the archenemies of her house, Capulet.
She responds by urging him, "Deny thy father and refuse thy
name," or to permit her to do that: "I'll no longer be a Capulet."
As the remainder of the play shows, Juliet's approach is tragically
naïve. Names matter.

The last chapter explored Jesus' identity as the Son of God.
That is his (and, as we'll see, our) "family name." Historically,
family names were a way of indicating who one's father was: this
is how we got names such as Stephenson and Paulson, MacGre-
gor (son of Gregor), and O'Neill (originally Ó Neill, meaning
"grandson of Neill"). Jesus is the Son of the Father, the Son of
God. In this chapter, we'll look at his first name, tracing the history of YHWH, Emmanuel, and Jesus.

The Unspeakable Name: YHWH

If Adam, in naming the animals in Genesis, implied his dominion over them — and (more controversially) if Adam's naming
of his wife indicates his headship even in regard to his equal —
then man clearly cannot name God. God must reveal his own
name to man. This is the drama at the heart of much of the Book
of Exodus. It is often overlooked amid the more engaging story
of Moses' leading the Israelites out of Egypt. But this naming
is a theme that unfolds amid the Exodus and inseparably from
it. The revelation of the divine name occurs during Moses' encounter with God in the burning bush:

> Then Moses said to God, "If I come to the people of Is-
> rael and say to them, 'The God of your fathers has sent
> me to you,' and they ask me, 'What is his name?' what
> shall I say to them?" God said to Moses, "I AM WHO I
> AM" [YHWH]. And he said, "Say this to the people of
> Israel, 'I am has sent me to you.'" God also said to Mo-
> ses, "Say this to the sons of Israel, 'The LORD [YHWH],
> the God of your fathers, the God of Abraham, the God

of Isaac, and the God of Jacob, has sent me to you': this
is my name for ever, and thus I am to be remembered
throughout all generations." (Exodus 3:13–15)

Unlike other names for God that are perhaps more properly
considered titles, the name YHWH appears to be something
like a proper name. Some have read God's reply as a refusal to
give a name[5] (something like "I am who I am, stop asking so
many questions!"), but that fits neither the context of Exodus 3
nor the broader biblical witness: "Our Redeemer — the LORD
[YHWH] of hosts is his name — is the Holy One of Israel" (Is
47:4); "the LORD [YHWH] the God of hosts, the LORD [YHWH]
is his name" (Hos 12:5); "the LORD [YHWH] is his name" (Am
9:6), and so forth.

But the divine name is much more than a name. As *The
Jewish Encyclopedia* explains, it "represents the Hebrew conception of the divine nature or character and of the relation of
God to His people. It represents the Deity as He is known to His
worshipers."[6] That's all well and good, but what does this name
mean? Attempts to trace the name to the name of some earlier deity in Indo-European, Old Babylonian, Arabic, Egyptian,
Amorite, or other language or culture have failed.[7] The God of
Israel very much appears to be something other than a warmed-
over retelling of ancient Near Eastern pagan myths. His name
comes from a Hebrew verb that can mean "to become" or "to
be." The meaning seems to be "I AM WHO AM" or, in the third
person, "He who is."

The name is enough to make a metaphysician's heart thrill.
Pagan Greek philosophers such as Plato (427–347 B.C.) and his
student Aristotle (384–322 B.C.) had started to recognize a gradation within existence. For example, does a shadow or a reflection exist? Sort of. We can speak intelligibly of shadows existing,
but outside of the whimsical world of *Peter Pan*, shadows aren't
beings, and they don't possess existence as beings do. Even within the realm of beings, we can speak of gradation. While admit-

ting of some confusing cases (a Venus flytrap appears to be more alive than a mollusk, for example), we can generally speak of an ascension in the order of being from lifeless things to plants, to animals, and eventually to humans.[8]

God's self-revelation as "I AM WHO AM" suggests that he is establishing himself on the top of this metaphysical food chain, as infinite and unbound existence. It's God saying that he is, as Saint Anselm would later describe him, "that than which a greater cannot be thought" (see chapter 1).[9] Perhaps that seems too abstract and philosophical. These were primitive people, recently freed from slavery. To this objection, E. C. B. MacLaurin reminds us that "the revelation was made to Moses, whose early upbringing had placed him in a different category from that of his followers.[10] In any case, much of the opposition on this front, as Dennis McCarthy points out, is rooted in a "silly Hebrew-Greek dichotomy"[11] — the false idea that all the smart, philosophical, academic things are Greek, and the Jews only have legalism and tribal religion.

The biblical evidence repeatedly treats God's name as meaning something like "He who exists." We see this in the Jewish oath "as YHWH lives," which we find repeatedly in the Old Testament (e.g., Jgs 8:19; Ru 3:13; 1 Sm 14:39, 45; Jer 4:2). But the clearest indication of the Jewish understanding of the divine name comes from the Book of Wisdom. The book is a part of the Catholic Old Testament but not the Protestant or modern Jewish canon. Significantly, it predates the birth of Christ, so (whatever one's views on its canonicity) it can hardly be accused of simply imposing Christian theology on Jewish thinking. In it, the author describes the foolishness of idolaters: "For all men who were ignorant of God were foolish by nature; and they were unable from the good things that are seen to know *him who exists*, nor did they recognize the craftsman while paying heed to his works" (Wis 13:1; emphasis added).[12] This description of God as "him who exists" or "he who exists" appears to be a literal Greek translation of YHWH.[13]

But the divine name seems to mean even more than this. Remember that the verb used means both "to be" and (in fact, more often) "to become." There's a sense not only of existence, but of activity. And this sense of divine action is present from God's first self-revelation to Moses, both with his command to tell the people, "I AM has sent me to you" and the promise immediately following it: "I have observed you and what has been done to you in Egypt; and I promise that I will bring you up out of the affliction of Egypt, to … a land flowing with milk and honey" (Ex 3:14, 16–17). McCarthy argues that it's precisely because YHWH "*is* above all others" that "this means active and helping, for being and acting effectively were not separated"; for "the one who is acts."[14] Matthew Levering similarly asserts that by "naming himself in these ways — first by means of the verb 'to be,' second by the name 'YHWH,' and third as 'the God of your fathers, the God of Abraham, the God of Isaac, the God of Jacob,' the God of Israel associates his historical salvific activity with his metaphysical reality."[15]

You may have noticed that after the first time God uses the divine name, the translators write it, not as "YHWH," or as "I AM WHO I AM," but as "the LORD" with "Lord" in small caps. Why is that? We've just heard what the name YHWH means, and it's not "the Lord." In fact, there's another word, *Adonai* (אֲדֹנָי) that does mean "the Lord" and is translated as such without small caps. This is standard practice in translating the Hebrew into other languages, and it highlights the controversy over the name of God.

At some point in Jewish history (scholars aren't sure when), it became forbidden to speak the name YHWH. An early Talmudic text endorses the practice of "greeting one's fellow with God's name" and cites as support Ruth 2:4, in which Boaz says to the reapers, "The LORD [YHWH] be with you!" and they answer, "The LORD [YHWH] bless you."[16] In a slightly later Talmudic text, dated to A.D. 190–230, the Jewish sage Abba Shaul warns that "one who utters the Divine Name as it is spelled" has "no share in the world to come."[17] And there is evidence suggesting that this practice of not speaking the divine name is much older, dating back to at least the time when 1 Chronicles was written, several centuries before the birth of Christ.[18]

In prayer, pious Jews use the word *Adonai* (Lord) in lieu of the ineffable name. Outside of prayer, they don't use even *Adonai*, instead using *HaShem* (the Name). As the Hebrew Scriptures were being translated into the Greek version of the Bible known as the Septuagint, perhaps around the third century B.C., translators tended to translate YHWH as *Kyrios* (Greek for "Lord") but declined it differently from the translation of *Adonai* (which actually means "Lord").[19] Even Jesus is depicted in the New Testament as following this practice. For instance, in Psalm 110:1, David says, "YHWH says to my lord," but in Matthew 22:44, when Jesus quotes the psalm, he says, "The Lord [*Kyrios*] said to my Lord." In fact, the name YHWH is never used directly by anyone in the New Testament. The use of LORD versus Lord in English is a sort of continuation of this custom.[20]

This refusal even to speak the name of God points to how seriously the Jews took the idea of the holiness of his name. We don't often consider how odd it is that on a list of only Ten Commandments, one of them is that "You shall not take the name of the LORD your God in vain; for the LORD will not hold him guiltless who takes his name in vain" (Ex 20:7). Not only is there a prohibition against using the Lord's name in vain, but this prohibition is so severe as to make the top-ten list. What does it mean to take the name of God in vain? Aquinas points to several ways: by blaspheming against the name (see Lv 24:16); by using it in a false oath or in an oath to do something wicked (see Lv 19:12); or by using it recklessly or frivolously, for example, by swearing by God's name over some trivial matter (see Sir 23:9).[21]

But the idea of taking the Lord's name in vain is much bigger than a literal reading might suggest. It means something closer to how we use it in the phrase "to damage one's good name." One's "name," in this case, is one's reputation. And so, arguably, one of the worst ways we can offend against the name of the Lord is through religious hypocrisy. Saint Paul seems to have this in view when he warns his Jewish readers, "You who boast in the law, do you dishonor God by breaking the law? For, as it is written, 'The name of God is blasphemed among the Gentiles because of you'" (Rom 2:23–24).

This broader sense is important for steering clear of legalism. If the commandment against taking the Lord's name in vain merely means not to use the name YHWH inappropriately, the best course of action is simply never to say the name, and forget the vowels. But God also says that "Our help is in the name of the LORD [YHWH], who made heaven and earth" (Ps 124:8) and that "it shall come to pass that all who call upon the name of the LORD [YHWH] shall be delivered" (Jl 2:32). It seems clear that he didn't reveal his name just for us to reconceal it in fear. But we ought to use the name of God when an oath is called for (as Saint Paul modeled in 2 Corinthians 1:23) or in specifically religious contexts, such as calling on the Trinity in baptism or in denouncing the devil.

Nevertheless, we are left with a divine name, the closest thing we have to a personal name for God, and we're not sure how to pronounce it. There's something strangely beautiful about that, as a character points out in *The Names of Christ* by Fray Luis de León (1527–1591):

> As you know, the name of God with four letters is a name that is not uttered, because vowels are not pronounced, because we do not know what their real sound should be, or because of the respect due to God, or else, as I have suspected sometimes, because it is like the mumbling sounds that a dumb person utters as an expression of friendship, affection, love: without a clear pattern, shapeless, as if God wanted us men to use as a word to express His infinite being a clumsy word or sound that would make us understand that God is too large to be

embraced or expressed in any clear way by our understanding and our tongue: Pronouncing such a name is
tantamount to admitting that we are limited and dumb
when we come face to face with God. Our confusion
and mumbling are a hymn of praise, as David declared;
the name of God is ineffable and unutterable.[22]

It's a reminder that we have, as chapter 1 pointed out, a "God
beyond all praising." No words, not even our clumsy prayers to
YHWH, do his infinite majesty justice.

The Name That Wasn't: Emmanuel

Without a doubt, the most famous Advent hymn is "O Come,
O Come Emmanuel." Many of us are familiar with the lyrics or
at least the refrain ("Rejoice, rejoice, Emmanuel shall come to
thee, O Israel!"). The seven verses of the hymn are poetic translations of the seven O Antiphons prayed at Vespers (Evening
Prayer) in the days leading up to Christmas, since at least the
eighth century.[23] Each is a title of Christ, such as Adonai, Root
of Jesse, Key of David, and of course, Emmanuel. But Emmanuel is the most obviously biblical title and simultaneously the
most confusing. It seems to say that the Messiah's name will be
Emmanuel (sometimes spelled "Immanuel"), yet we apply it to
a Messiah named Jesus. The biblical context we need to digest
is Isaiah 7:10–17, a dialogue between God, through the prophet
Isaiah, and King Ahaz of Judah. To do that, a bit of historical
background is necessary.

In the period during which Isaiah is writing, the twelve
tribes of Israel have split into two kingdoms and are at war with
each other. The northern ten tribes have rejected the Davidic
line of kings and have taken the name "the Kingdom of Israel" (although historians tend to refer to them as "the Northern
Kingdom" or as "Ephraim," from the location of their capital).
Their capital city was Samaria, which is why it's also called "Israel in Samaria" (see 1 Kgs 16:29) and why the descendants of

these tribes become known as the Samaritans. What about the southern two tribes? They become known as "the Kingdom of Judah" — again, after the location of their capital. The people in the south go from being called "Israelites" to being called "Jews" (from *Judah*).

Ahaz, the southern king, is a descendant of David and Solomon, but he's not a faithful Jew. Like many of the rulers from this period, he's overly influenced by the culture and religion of Judah's pagan neighbors, who often engaged in human sacrifice. 2 Kings 16:2–3 says that King Ahaz "did not do what was right in the eyes of the LORD his God, as his father David had done." Instead, he lived like "the kings of Israel" (meaning the corrupt Samaritan kings), and he "even burned his son as an offering [literally, "made his son to pass through the fire"] according to the abominable practices of the nations whom the LORD drove out before the people of Israel."

Under King Ahaz, Judah is at war with "two smoldering stumps of firebrands" (Is 7:4), the Syrians and Samaritan Israelites. Ahaz is tempted to turn for help to another powerful pagan nation, the Assyrian Empire. God sends Isaiah to offer Ahaz relief, encouraging him to put his trust in the Lord rather than in the Assyrians. The king won't accept this divine overture. He says, "I am your servant and your son. Come up, and rescue me from the hand of the king of Syria and from the hand of the king of Israel, who are attacking me" (2 Kgs 16:7). This would make a beautiful prayer, except that it's directed to the King of Assyria rather than to the God of Israel. This turns out to be a crushing mistake. The Assyrians are only too happy to come, and they destroy both Samaria and Syria. But then they turn their attention toward Judah, taking some of the Jewish people into captivity and nearly destroying the Southern Kingdom as well as the Northern. Judah is only narrowly saved, due to the fidelity of King Hezekiah (Ahaz's son) a generation later. But we'll get to that.

First, what are the details of God's offer to Ahaz? Any sign he wants: "Ask a sign of the LORD your God; let it be deep as Sheol or high as heaven." This is the sort of thing so many people wish they could get from God. It's a mark of how corrupt Ahaz is that he refuses, under the guise of false piety. He says, "I will not ask, and I will not put the LORD to the test." The prophetic response is the now-famous Christmas proclamation: "Hear then, O house of David! Is it too little for you to weary men, that you weary my God also? Therefore the LORD himself will give you a sign" (Is 7:11–13). This is addressed to King Ahaz as the "House of David," suggesting why God offers to intervene on the unworthy king's behalf: to preserve the royal Davidic lineage.

What is the sign to be given by YHWH? A maiden (`almah, עַלְמָה) "shall conceive and bear a son, and shall call his name Immanuel" (Is 7:14). Before we get into the meaning of *Emmanuel*, we need to explore the meaning of `almah. There's some debate over whether this is a prophecy of the Virgin Birth (or even a virginal birth at all), because of God's use of this word. Until fairly recently, Christian Bibles (following Matthew 1:23) translated it as "virgin," but some modern Bibles, including the Revised Standard Version, now translate it as "young woman" instead. Why?

The Hebrew word *na`arah* (נַעֲרָה) meant "young woman" with no implication of virginity. In Amos 2:7, the word is used to describe prostitutes. Another word, *běthuwlah* (בְּתוּלָה), meant "virgin," but with no suggestion of youth. It's used to refer to the deceased virgin sisters of Jewish priests (Lv 21:3). But God uses neither of those; instead, he uses `almah, עַלְמָה, which suggests both youth and virginity. In an age in which young, unmarried women (excluding prostitutes) could be presumed to be virgins, it made sense for one word to carry both senses. This is exactly the dual meaning of the English word *maiden* (from the Old English *mæden*). So the most literal translation would be something like "a maiden shall conceive and bear a son." But the implication of virginity was understood and was crucial to the miraculous nature of the sign.

If you read the New Testament, you'll find that this is exactly how Saint Matthew treats the prophecy: as saying that a "virgin shall conceive and bear" (1:23). Matthew was hardly the first to read it this way. Centuries earlier, when the Jewish Septuagint (the Greek text of the Old Testament) was created, the translators opted for the word *parthenos* (παρθένος), "virgin," suggesting that they understood the prophecy the same way. And reasonably so. Remember the context: God is promising an astounding sign, as high as the heavens or as low as the netherworld. Ahaz is being told of a miracle that will seemingly surpass all other miracles. Childbirth in the ordinary course of nature, while beautiful, doesn't fit that bill. A virgin birth, on the other hand, does — particularly if it's the virgin birth of YHWH himself.

To whom does this prophecy refer? Scholars, particularly those skeptical of the New Testament (or who seek another fulfillment of the prophecy) tend to find this passage "especially troublesome," with commentators coming up "not only with differing positions on almost every point, but often with positions that are diametrically opposed."[24] Let's consider a few of the proposed candidates.

Isaiah's Wife and Son

In one interpretation, the "maiden" is Isaiah's own prophetess wife, and the child is his son, Maher-Shalal-Hash-Baz, conceived and born in Isaiah 8.[25] The best argument for this theory is that, in the very next chapter, Isaiah's wife "conceived and bore a son" (Is 8:3) named Maher-Shalal-Hash-Baz. Like Emmanuel, Isaiah and his sons are described as "signs" (Is 8:18), and the wording and content of the warnings are remarkably similar. Isaiah 7:16 prophesies that before Emmanuel "knows how to refuse the evil and choose the good, the land before whose two kings you are in dread will be deserted," and Isaiah 8:4 prophesies that before Maher-Shalal-Hash-Baz "knows how to cry 'My father' or 'My mother,' the wealth of Damascus and the spoil of Samaria will be carried away before the king of Assyria."

Both Emmanuel and Maher-Shalal-Hash-Baz are present-ed as signs that Damascus (Syria) and Samaria are going to fall, but the two signs mean very different things. Isaiah's son's name means "speeding to the plunder, hurrying to the spoil" and is an ominous sign that the Assyrians are coming, not just for Judah's enemies, but for Judah itself.[26] The significance of the name is not that "God is with us" but that Assyria is coming.

Moreover, Isaiah's wife cannot be the *'almah* of the proph-ecy, because she is apparently neither young nor a virgin. Isaiah has been a prophet during the reigns of three kings by the time of the Isaiah 7 prophecy (see Is 1:1), so it is unlikely that his wife is a young maiden. More to the point, Isaiah already has a son (Is 7:3), and "a woman is not called *'almah* after her first preg-nancy."[27] Some proponents of this theory try to get around these difficulties by imagining that Isaiah's older son is the child of another woman, perhaps a now-deceased first wife,[28] but noth-ing in the text suggests this. A theory that requires adding coun-terintuitive details to the text (e.g., Isaiah's son isn't his wife's son) indicates poor exegesis.

King Ahaz's Wife and Son

The theory that the text refers to King Ahaz's wife and son ini-tially makes sense.[29] After all, the prophecy is being made to Ahaz, who is addressed in his capacity as representative of the "House of David" (Is 7:2, 13). Plus, it's through Ahaz's son Heze-kiah (the continuation of the Davidic line) that God repels the Assyrian invaders. Unlike his father, Hezekiah is a faithful king of Judah, turning the peoples' hearts toward God and turning back the Assyrian invaders. He reminds the people, and is him-self a reminder to the people, that God is still with them.

This was a popular Jewish interpretation. Saint Justin Mar-tyr mentions in his *Dialogue with Trypho* that his Jewish inter-locutor claimed that the Isaiah 7 prophecy is best translated as "the young woman [rather than 'the virgin'] shall conceive," and that "the whole prophecy refers to Hezekiah."[30] So high was the

Jewish opinion of Hezekiah that many viewed him as a possibility for the Messiah. The Jewish Talmud goes so far as to claim that God "wished to appoint Hezekiah as the Messiah" but couldn't (due to his own just nature), because Hezekiah failed to offer any psalms of praise despite the miracles wrought through him.[31]

There are a few critical flaws in this interpretation. King Ahaz wasn't eagerly longing for a male heir to the royal lineage. Remember, he was quite willing to sacrifice one of his royal sons to Baal. But there's a bigger, mathematical problem. Ahaz was king of Israel for sixteen years (2 Kgs 16:2; 2 Chr 28:1), at which point the crown passed to his twenty-five-year-old son, Hezekiah (2 Kgs 18:1–2; 2 Chr 29:1), meaning that Hezekiah was about nine years old when his father took the throne, and may have been ruling alongside his father at the time of the Isaiah 7 prophecy.[32] The prophecy of the coming birth of Emmanuel could not be about the birth of the already-born Hezekiah.

An Unknown Woman and Child

According to another theory, "Isaiah most likely signified an unmarried young woman within the royal house, one known to Ahaz."[33] This theory requires assuming several details neither mentioned in nor suggested by the text: that there was some woman within the royal court, known to King Ahaz but not known to us; that Isaiah pointed her out or otherwise signified her to Ahaz; and that this woman conceived and bore a son named Emmanuel. But scriptural exegesis never hinges on inventing these sorts of crucial facts. In some variations of this theory, the woman is a virgin, meaning that we have to assume yet another crucial detail: that shortly after this prophecy, there's a virgin birth that neither Isaiah nor anyone else bothers to record.

In other variations of this theory, there's not even a virgin birth: it's just a young woman who gives birth in the ordinary course of nature, and names her baby Emmanuel.[34] But as J. Alec Motyer quite reasonably asks, "Where is the 'sign quality' in this

— especially after Isaiah has spoken the name and set the idea in motion?"[35] There's nothing miraculous about the pregnancy, and nothing miraculous about the choice of name.[36] In no way does it constitute a miraculous sign as "deep as Sheol or high as heaven" (Is 7:11).

None of these theories, then, works particularly well. It would be easy to assume that the only reason anyone favors such theories is hostility to Christianity — that they'll accept anything, so long as it isn't the Gospel. But such a view is too cynical, since even many Christian exegetes misread the Emmanuel passage in these ways. A better explanation is that they share a common presupposition that "a sign must function in its immediate circumstances or it has no sign-value."[37] According to this view, "the circumstances surrounding the prophecy demand a more immediate fulfillment" than the birth of Christ, because the Davidic line was in danger of expiring, and the passage "indicates that a child would be born in the days of Ahaz who would serve as a sign to that generation of God's providential control of international events and of His people's destiny."[38]

From a human point of view, that makes a certain amount of sense. But God's signs don't always work that way. When God sends Moses to bring his people out of Egypt, he promises a sign of sorts: "I will be with you; and this shall be the sign for you, that I have sent you: when you have brought forth the people out of Egypt, you shall serve God upon this mountain" (Ex 3:12). Moses won't be able to see the sign until after he trusts in God and delivers his people from slavery.

But even from a human perspective, we often act toward goals that won't be immediately realizable. In 1862, President Abraham Lincoln says to a crowd gathered in Frederick, Maryland, that he wishes that "our children and our children's children to a thousand generations" would "continue to enjoy the benefits conferred upon us by a united country."[39] That is, one of his motives for continuing to fight the arduous Civil War is his desire to secure the nation for a thousand generations after his death.

Likewise, God promises the original Abraham that his descendants would be as numerous as the stars (Gn 15:5). Neither the president nor the patriarch believed that he would be around to see the events he hoped for, but that's the point: They strive for something that would last long after them. The Old Testament Abraham is confident, even when it seems that his son Isaac will die at his own hands, that everything will somehow turn out right. Why? Because if God's far-off prophecy is true, the story can't be over in Abraham's immediate generation. In the words of Hebrews 11:17–19:

> By faith Abraham, when he was tested, offered up Isaac, and he who had received the promises was ready to offer up his only-begotten son, of whom it was said, "Through Isaac shall your descendants be named." He considered that God was able to raise men even from the dead; hence he did receive him back, and this was a symbol.

In other words, it's good that these signs are in the distant future. If Abraham, Moses, and the Davidic kings trust God, they can rest secure that, no matter how dark things get, the story isn't over at least until the pending prophecies are fulfilled. If you've never seen the *Rocky* movies, but know that there's a *Rocky III*, you don't have to worry that Rocky is going to die in the first one. But if you're watching the last movie in the series, you don't know ahead of time whether the protagonist will die in it. Had the Emmanuel prophecy been fulfilled in Ahaz's lifetime, or the mountain prophecy fulfilled before the Exodus, there would be less cause for security.

From a human perspective, we want God's signs here and now, for God to prove himself and his promises to us. But God often makes us wait for his miraculous signs, such that we can receive the promise of them only in faith. To a faithless king such as Ahaz, the Emmanuel prophecy probably meant nothing. To his faithful son Hezekiah, on the other hand, it was a source of strength and hope. Rallying Judah to fight the Assyrians, Hezekiah encouraged them: "Be strong and of good courage. Do not be afraid or dismayed before the king of Assyria and all the horde that is with him; for there is one greater with us than with him. With him is an arm of flesh; but with us is the LORD our God, to help us and to fight our battles" (2 Chr 32:7–8).

Hezekiah is reminding his men that the Assyrians have the earthly power, but Israel has "God with us," Emmanuel.[40] By receiving the prophecy in faith, believing that God continues to be with his people even amid the darkness of the present hour, Hezekiah has the trusting confidence missing from his father (and many modern scholars). And so we must ultimately conclude that the Emmanuel passage is, in the words of Benedict XVI, "a word in waiting" to be received in faith, and that there "is nothing in its own historical context to correspond to it."[41]

The Name above All Names: Jesus Christ

There's one last interpretation of the Emmanuel prophecy to consider, and we find it in the Infancy Narratives. The angel Gabriel is sent by God "to a city of Galilee named Nazareth, to a virgin betrothed to a man whose name was Joseph, of the house of David; and the virgin's name was Mary" (Lk 1:26–27). The promise to the Davidic line is finally coming true, but not through a queen in a palace in Jerusalem. Instead, Emmanuel will arrive through a young Jewish virgin girl descended from royalty long ago. Gabriel's message is shocking: "Do not be afraid, Mary, for you have found favor with God. And behold, you will conceive in your womb and bear a son, and you shall call his name Jesus" (Lk 1:30–31). Both Gabriel's message to Mary and the angelic message to Joseph include the same curious detail: a command to name the child Jesus (see Mt 1:21). The name, in other words, is not an incidental detail. Yet Matthew is also quite clear that "all this took place to fulfil what the Lord had spoken by the prophet: 'Behold, a virgin shall conceive and bear a son, and his name shall be called Emmanuel'" (1:22–23).

Many Christians simply don't understand what the evangelists are saying in the Infancy Narratives. For example, Matthew mentions that Mary's husband Joseph "knew her not until she had borne a son" (1:25). Some readers, especially since the Reformation, have read this as suggestive of Joseph and Mary having been sexually active on or after Christmas Day. Such a reading totally misses Matthew's point.[42] He isn't trying to say anything one way or another about sexual activity between Joseph and Mary after the birth of Christ. Why would he? His focus is on the period up to the birth of Christ, and for a very specific reason.

When we moderns hear the prophecy that a virgin will "conceive and bear" a child, we treat the verbs as redundant, but they're not. There's a long period of time between conception and childbirth, as any pregnant woman can tell you. Matthew recognizes Isaiah 7:14 as a double prophecy: a virgin conceives and a virgin bears a child. The prophecy can't be fulfilled by a virgin losing her virginity and conceiving. And it's not enough that Mary be a virgin at the start of the pregnancy; she needs to be a virgin until the very end, if her child is to be the foretold Emmanuel. That's why Matthew makes a point of saying that Mary is a virgin until the birth of Christ: he's showing us that Jesus fulfills all of the Isaiah 7 prophecy.[43]

So, Saint Matthew is showing (a) that Jesus is the fulfillment of Emmanuel, (b) that the Messiah's name is Jesus, not Emmanuel, and (c) that this wasn't a mistake or an incidental detail. This is confusing, since Isaiah clearly says that the woman "shall call his name Immanuel" (Is 7:14). But it's not an uncommon feature for Messianic prophecies to read this way. For example, God says through the prophet Zechariah, "Behold, the man whose name is the Branch: for he shall grow up in his place, and he shall build the temple of the LORD" (6:12), and virtually no one has read that as meaning the Messiah's name should literally be Branch. Even the weak interpretations of Isaiah 7 (e.g., Maher-Shalal-Hash-Baz) tend to recognize that Isaiah isn't talking about someone literally named Emmanuel.

So not only is the fulfillment of the Emmanuel prophecy not someone literally named Emmanuel, but it was important enough for the Messiah's name to be Jesus that this was the subject of two angelic visitations (see Mt 1:21; Lk 1:31). This is the first biblical clue that there's power in the name of Jesus, but hardly the last. In Mark 9:38–41, we hear of people, including non-Christians, casting out demons in the name of Jesus. Saint Peter, encountering a lame beggar, says to him, "I have no silver and gold, but I give you what I have; in the name of Jesus Christ of Nazareth, walk" (Acts 3:6). The Jewish Sanhedrin then demands to know, "By what power or by what name did you do this?", to which Peter indelicately replies that it was "by the name of Jesus Christ of Nazareth, whom you crucified, whom God raised from the dead." He then proceeds to say that "there is salvation in no one else, for there is no other name under heaven given among men by which we must be saved" (Acts 4:7, 10, 12). Saint Paul reminds the Colossians, "whatever you do, in word or deed, do everything in the name of the Lord Jesus, giving thanks to God the Father through him" (Col 3:17), and he speaks to the Corinthians of having "pronounced judgment in the name of the Lord Jesus" on a particularly sexually immoral man (1 Cor 5:3–4). Saint John summarizes the Father's commandment as "we should believe in the name of his Son Jesus Christ and love one another, just as he has commanded us" (1 Jn 3:23).

It would be easy to take these passages legalistically, as referring literally to the syllables of the name Jesus, or at least the original Hebrew or Greek version of the name. Oneness Pentecostals, who deny the Holy Trinity, argue that baptisms must be done "in the name of Jesus," based on a literalistic reading of Acts 2:38, 8:16, 10:48, and 19:5. They refuse to baptize "in the name of the Father and of the Son and of the Holy Spirit," as Jesus commands in Matthew 28:19, because they "regard Jesus as the only saving name and the one name that encompasses God's redemptive work as Father, Son, and Spirit."[44] This is a disastrous misunderstanding. A hyperliteralistic reading ends up being self-refuting: Each of the aforementioned verses in Acts refers to baptism "in the name of Jesus Christ," and *Christ* (Anointed One) is a title, not a name. Attempts to read Scripture in this way lead to a rejection of the Trinity and a rejection of the baptismal formula explicitly given by Jesus Christ.

What the Jews and the early Christians meant by *name* is clear from the Sanhedrin's question to Peter: "By what power or by what name did you do this?" It's the same sense as when lawyers today speak of "acting in one's own name" or "acting in the name of someone else," meaning to act on your own or another's authority.[45] To put your trust "in the name of Jesus" is to trust not a word but a person.

That said, it's still important to point out that one of the ways we express our love and affection and trust is precisely with names. Olly Murs, the former *X Factor* presenter, described "the worst date I ever went on" as one in which he forgot his date's name. The result? The date "went down like a lead balloon."[46] Forgetting the employer, or the favorite food, or the number of siblings of a date is one thing; but forgetting a date's name seems like a personal affront. There's something intimate about a name. Some of the people in heaven (for example, the ones who died before the first Christmas) were saved despite their not knowing the literal name of Jesus. After all, Jesus hadn't been named yet. Yet these people were still saved by him, which is the sense in which Peter obviously meant his statement (otherwise, he would be condemning everyone prior to his own generation). But we have a gift, given to us through the Incarnation, that our ancestors didn't have: We can call upon Jesus by name.

Of course, such a suggestion would sound blasphemous to a first-century Jew. Why were the followers of Christ claiming that there was no other name by which to be saved besides Jesus? Why not besides the name of the God of Israel? We'll explore that in the next chapter, as we look at the relationship between the three names YHWH, Emmanuel, and Jesus. But for now, we should take our cue from Saint Joseph. There's a common claim that "there are no words of St. Joseph recorded in the Gospel,"[47] but that's not quite true. Although it's true that we have no direct quotations from Joseph, we know of exactly one word that he said. At the insistence of the angel (Mt 1:21), it is he who had the honor of officially naming his foster son, and so it is he who first "called his name Jesus" (Mt 1:25). If you're remembered for nothing else in this life, if your words are lost to history and only one thing remains, let it be for calling on Jesus.

CHAPTER 4
Jesus, Lord and God

So who is Jesus, and what is his relationship to YHWH? If the heart of Christianity is the question "Who is Jesus?," then the core of that question is "What is his relationship to YHWH?" This is the thrust of Jesus' questions to the disciples: "Who do men say that the Son of man is?" and "Who do you say that I am?" (Mt 16:13, 15). Various thinkers, and various religious systems, have attempted to find the answer.

How did the crowds at the time of Christ view him? In response to the first of his two questions, the disciples replied, "Some say John the Baptist, others say Elijah, and others Jeremiah or one of the prophets" (Mt 16:14). Again, these responses are strange to us: Elijah, Jeremiah, and John the Baptist were dead by this point. There are two ways of making sense of this. One is that the crowds meant this figuratively or in a purely spiritual way. Elijah's disciple Elisha, knowing that his master was going to be taken up into heaven, prayed, "Let me inherit a double share of your spirit." Afterward, the other prophets recognized that "the spirit of Elijah rests on Elisha," and Elisha ended up performing twice as many miracles as his teacher had (see 2 Kgs 2:9, 15). But the crowds may have meant their belief more literally: Elijah never died but was assumed into heaven (2 Kgs 2:11), and many Jews awaited his bodily return to earth. King Herod, perhaps grief-stricken over having the man killed, suggested to his servants that Jesus was "John the Baptist; he has been raised from the dead; that is why these powers are at work in him" (Mt 14:1–2). All of this is to say that popular opinion recognized in Jesus human wisdom coupled with divine knowledge and even something otherworldly. But no one suggested that Jesus was YHWH.

Many modern thinkers agree with the crowds. The psychiatrist and philosopher Karl Jaspers (1883–1969) described Jesus, Socrates, Buddha, and Confucius as "paradigmatic individuals" who grew from historical figures into "mythical archetypes."[1] In this view, Jesus is only "one element in the Biblical religion" and isn't the founder of Christianity. Instead, "the reality of Jesus was overlaid by ideas that were alien to him," and he was "transformed from Jesus to Christ, the Son of God, from a human reality to an object of faith."[2] Similarly, the Jehovah's Witnesses teach that it's a myth that Jesus is God and that "religion actually degrades Jesus when it teaches that he was God in the flesh."[3] Instead, he is merely someone who "became the wisest man ever to walk the earth."[4] There's something inescapably attractive about Jesus, something that draws even many ardent nonbelievers, and the "brilliant wise man" answer allows one to esteem Jesus and his teachings without believing him to be God.

Jesus' Divine Claims

Did Jesus present himself as divine? Yes, both in his spoken claims and in his actions. What he said and what he did are inseparable. For example, Jesus "called the twelve together and gave them power and authority over all demons and to cure diseases, and he sent them out to preach the kingdom of God and to heal" (Lk 9:1–2). Is this an action or a claim? Both. Jesus' action of giving the Twelve this "power and authority" implies a claim about himself: namely, that he has this power to give. Soon after, John returns to report, "We saw a man casting out demons in your name," to which Jesus replies not to forbid him (see Lk 9:49). Yet neither John nor Jesus seems to find it odd that demons are being driven out in Jesus' name.

Then there is the almost offhanded way in which Jesus re-fers to himself as the Lord who will come to judge the living and the dead on the Last Day: "Not every one who says to me, 'Lord, Lord,' shall enter the kingdom of heaven, but he who does the will of my Father who is in heaven. On that day many will say to me, 'Lord, Lord, did we not prophesy in your name, and cast out demons in your name, and do many mighty works in your name?' And then will I declare to them, 'I never knew you; de-part from me, you evildoers'" (Mt 7:21–23).

Note well that Jesus' "I never knew you" is enough to send a person to hell. Do these sound like the words of an ordinary prophet or teacher? Can you imagine Jeremiah or Gandhi say-ing that unless he knows us personally, we cannot be saved? And what's more, even the good works that Jesus points to — feeding the hungry, clothing the naked, and the like — he applied to himself, saying, "As you did it to one of the least of these my brethren, you did it to me" (Mt 25:40). Christ is presenting him-self as present in the poor and the marginalized in a way that only God could be.

One Sabbath, Jesus and his disciples were going through fields of grain, "and as they made their way his disciples began to pluck heads of grain" (Mk 2:23). This activity is explicitly permitted by Deuteronomy: "When you go into your neigh-bor's standing grain, you may pluck the ears with your hand, but you shall not put a sickle to your neighbor's standing grain" (Dt 23:25). Nevertheless, the Pharisees rebuked them, accusing them of violating the Sabbath. Hadn't God said to Moses, "Six days you shall work, but on the seventh day you shall rest; in plowing time and in harvest you shall rest" (Ex 34:21)? But of course, only the most legalistic of minds could consider the dis-ciples' plucking to be harvesting.

So we might expect Jesus simply to call them from the letter of their interpretation to the spirit of the law itself. And he does this, reminding them that "the sabbath was made for man, not man for the sabbath" (Mk 2:27). Likewise, on another occasion, he asked them, "Is it lawful on the sabbath to do good or to do harm, to save life or to destroy it?" to explain why it was lawful for him to heal people miraculously on the Sabbath (see Lk 6:9). But he ultimately grounds his ability to interpret what does and doesn't violate Sabbath rest in the fact that "the Son of man is lord of the sabbath" (Mt 12:8; Mk 2:28; Lk 13:15). He even compared the disciples with him to the priests who guiltlessly "worked" in the Temple on the Sabbath, saying "I tell you, something greater than the temple is here" (Mt 12:6). None of the prophets ever claimed to be greater than the Temple, or claimed to be Lord of the Sabbath. Such things were divine claims, and Saint John explains that this "was why the Jews sought all the more to kill him, because he not only broke the sabbath but also called God his Father, making himself equal with God" (Jn 5:18).

As C. S. Lewis famously pointed out in *Mere Christianity*, Jesus is either the God he claims to be, or a liar pretending to be God, or a quite delusional madman.[5] But whichever of these he is, he cannot be reduced to merely a "great teacher" or "paradigmatic individual." Depending on whether his claims are true, he's either so much more or so much less than that.

It's not difficult to choose between these three options. Jesus' character in the Gospel is humble, and his teachings are insightful. To be sure, history bears witness to no shortage of con men and grifters, charlatans and madmen, but they bear little resemblance to Jesus of Nazareth. This is precisely why even those who reject his divine claims still want to hold on to him as a "great teacher," in a way that they wouldn't for a lunatic or a con artist. It's also worth pointing out here that the Twelve Apostles spent three years with Jesus and came away apparently convinced that the man was sinless. Consider anyone you've lived with for more than a few days, such as a roommate or a spouse — how likely were either of you to conclude that the other was wholly without sin? And so, the reasonable conclusion is the one Lewis comes to: "It seems to me obvious that He was neither a lunatic nor a fiend: and consequently, however strange or terrifying or unlikely it may seem, I have to accept the view that He was and is God."[6]

The Reliability of the Apostles

Lewis's "trilemma" — that Jesus is either Lord, liar, or lunatic — leaves open one other possibility: legend. The view of Jaspers, as we've seen, is that Jesus didn't originally make the sort of divine claims that the Bible ascribes to him. Or, to put it another way, Lewis's argument is an airtight case for the divinity of Christ if and only if we can trust the biblical account.

Can we trust the original witness of the apostles? As a former attorney, I know a couple of helpful questions to consider in assessing witness testimony: "Is the person in a position to know the truth?" and "Does the person have a motive to lie?" A person may tell the truth as best he knows it but still be misinformed. When I point out that the apostles wouldn't have been willingly martyred for a lie, people not infrequently respond with, "But what about Muslim suicide bombers? Don't they die for a false religion?" But these modern-day adherents to Islam have no way of knowing whether Muhammad was telling the truth. They're simply taking his word for it. Even if they are acting in good faith, that doesn't mean their prophet did. The apostles were in a different position. By their own testimony, they were in a position to know the truth about Jesus' death and resurrection. They claim not just to have heard about it but to have conversed with the risen Christ at various points over the course of forty days (see Acts 1:3-4). So the apostles meet the first of these two criteria. The only question, then, is whether they and Jesus were telling the truth.

It's certainly true that people make false religious claims, and many of them seem to make these claims knowingly — that is, they lie. There are usually obvious motives for making such claims. Take, for example, Muhammad, the founder of Islam; Joseph Smith, the founder of Mormonism; and David Koresh, the leader of the infamous Branch Davidians. Each of those putative prophets claimed that God had permitted or even ordered him to have sex with a variety of women and underage girls.[7]

Additionally, each man raised an army of sorts. Muhammad's was a wildly successful army, creating an empire that covered the entire Arabian peninsula by the time of his death.[8] Joseph Smith allegedly threatened to "trample down our enemies and make it one gore of blood from the Rocky Mountains to the Atlantic Ocean," and to "be to this generation a second Mohammed, whose motto in treating for peace was 'the Alcoran [Qur'an] or the Sword.' So shall it eventually be with us — 'Joseph Smith or the Sword!'"[9] But although his ambition may have matched Muhammad's, his military prowess did not, despite his having formed a 5,000-man militia. After Smith had a hostile newspaper shut down and its press destroyed, the State of Illinois brought their own militia and had Smith and other Mormon leaders arrested.[10] An anti-Mormon mob attacked the prison, and Smith faced off against them by firing a pistol he had smuggled in. Attempting to escape through a prison window, he was shot and killed. Koresh, too, died by the sword, as anyone who watched the news in the early 1990s may recall.

Contrast these lives and deaths with those of Jesus and the apostles. What's striking is precisely the refusal of Jesus or his followers to seize power or claim special sexual privileges. As Saint Peter said to Jesus, "Behold, we have left everything and followed you" (Mk 10:28; cf. Lk 18:28). Jesus responded, "Truly, I say to you, there is no man who has left house or wife or brothers or parents or children, for the sake of the kingdom of God, who will not receive manifold more in this time, and in the age to come eternal life" (Lk 18:29–30; cf. Mk 10:29–30). From Jesus' response, it seems clear that the Twelve gave up not only material possessions but even the possibility of family life. The rest of the New Testament corroborates this: There's no record that any of the apostles had any wives, much less a multitude of them, at the time.[11] The closest we get is a reference to Peter having a mother-in-law (see Mt 8:14–15), but there's no reference to a living wife, and the life of itinerant preaching to which Jesus called the

Twelve seems prohibitive of domestic bliss. In response to a man who wanted to follow him, Jesus warned, "Foxes have holes, and birds of the air have nests; but the Son of man has nowhere to lay his head" (Lk 9:58).

Unlike Muhammad, Smith, and Koresh, Jesus and the apostles didn't engage in armed resistance. Even at Jesus' arrest, when "Simon Peter, having a sword, drew it and struck the high priest's slave and cut off his right ear" (Jn 18:10), Jesus healed the man's ear (see Lk 22:51), and rebuked Peter by saying that "all who take the sword will perish by the sword" (Mt 26:52). Nor was Jesus an unwilling martyr, as even the critics of Christianity implicitly concede. For instance, the Talmud says that "the gentile authorities were interested in his acquittal. Consequently, the court gave him every opportunity to clear himself, so that it could not be claimed that he was falsely convicted."[12] Pontius Pilate in particular was a reluctant participant in the death of Christ. His death, in other words, was hardly unavoidable, as he elsewhere acknowledged: "I lay down my life, that I may take it again. No one takes it from me, but I lay it down of my own accord" (Jn 10:17–18). He made this point expressly to Peter, explaining the absurdity of resisting martyrdom with violence: "Do you think that I cannot appeal to my Father, and he will at once send me more than twelve legions of angels? But how then should the scriptures be fulfilled, that it must be so?" (Mt 26:53–54). The martyrdoms of Jesus and his apostles look very different from the armed-prison-break "martyrdom" of Smith, or the hostage taking and fifty-four-day federal standoff of Koresh.

Recall that the apostles, like Jesus, were Jews. This is an obvious point, but one we often overlook. The Jews were fiercely monotheistic, such that Saul (the future Saint Paul) and others were seeking to have the Christians killed for proclaiming what they viewed as heretical doctrine. The disciples knew that following Christ meant social and even familial ostracization; Jesus warned them directly, saying that he had "come to set a man against his father, and a daughter against her mother, and a daughter-in-law against her mother-in-law; and a man's foes will be those of his own household" (Mt 10:35–36). But the suffering they experienced was more than simply ostracization: it regularly included beatings, whippings, and imprisonment. To get a sense of the life of an apostle, consider Saint Paul's description:

> Five times I have received at the hands of the Jews the forty lashes less one. Three times I have been beaten with rods; once I was stoned. Three times I have been shipwrecked; a night and a day I have been adrift at sea; on frequent journeys, in danger from rivers, danger from robbers, danger from my own people, danger from Gentiles, danger in the city, danger in the wilderness, danger at sea, danger from false brethren; in toil and hardship, through many a sleepless night, in hunger and thirst, often without food, in cold and exposure. And, apart from other things, there is the daily pressure upon me of my anxiety for all the churches. Who is weak, and I am not weak? Who is made to fall, and I am not indignant? (2 Corinthians 11:24–29)

At the end of such a life, the apostles could reasonably predict that they would end up being martyred by either Jewish leaders (who viewed them as heretics) or the Roman government (who viewed them as subversive criminals). And indeed, only John escaped this fate. In the words of Josh D. McDowell, "Many people have died for a lie, but they did so believing it was the truth," and it "would be hard to find a group of men anywhere in history who would die for a lie if they knew it was a lie."[13]

But here's where the Jewish perspective becomes important: after death, it only gets worse. In our times, we've largely lost anything like a serious belief in hell. But the early followers of Christ took the idea of hell quite seriously. If the apostles were lying, they spent their entire lives proclaiming idolatry and could expect to spend eternity in agony. Indeed, the Jewish Talmud claims that Jesus is spending eternity in the next world, "sentenced to boiling excrement," for mocking "the words of the Sages."[14] That's an ugly claim, but it highlights how seriously the Jews took religious transgressions. That's what Jesus and the apostles were facing. And what's more, these men wouldn't be damning just themselves — they would be taking along with them as many of their friends and loved ones as possible.

Whatever one's beliefs, it's at least easy to understand why Muhammad, Joseph Smith, or David Koresh might have had incentive to lie or at least to take their ideas as coming from God. But what would motivate someone like Saul of Tarsus to give up a promising rabbinical career in order to promote a blasphemous lie, all so he could endure the kind of suffering he described in 2 Corinthians 11:24–29, only to spend eternity roasting in his own excrement? There's ultimately no coherent reason to believe that the apostles were lying, unless one starts from the perspective that the Gospel accounts can't be true; and we know from the apostles' testimony that they couldn't have been innocently misinformed in the way someone relaying secondhand information might. They were reporting eyewitness testimony and were absolutely adamant about its veracity. The most logical thing to do is to believe them.

The Reliability of the Copyists

But can we trust that this original, reliable witness of the apostles hasn't been corrupted over the course of the last twenty centuries?

A great many scholarly theories speculate that certain parts of the biblical text belong to the original authors, while other parts are later interpolations created to fit the theological needs of the contemporary community. This is, however, fundamentally unserious scholarship and terrible theology. Mark Shea has traced the history of what he calls the "Latest Real Jesus," in which a never-ending series of popular authors "discover" a Jesus who always looks a great deal like the Jesus of each author's own imagination or the popular culture of the day.[15] Everyone from Social Gospel Protestants to avowed capitalists to Nazis to Marxists proclaimed that the "real" Jesus happened to believe just what they believe. This has continued down through the ages (remember *Jesus Christ Superstar* and the homosexual play *Corpus Christi*), as men never cease to remake Jesus in their own image and likeness.

Academic scholars, sadly, can't seem to resist this impulse. Two decades ago, Joseph Sievers traced the history of scholarship on Jesus throughout the twentieth century, and it looked much like the history of the popular authors Shea describes. Among these scholars, there has been an elaboration of "a series of criteria to establish with more surety which sayings of the Gospel can be attributed to Jesus himself."[16] While there is no unanimity, one of the standard criteria is the principle of dissimilarity, meaning that "if a saying is 'dissimilar' from the interests both of the primitive Christian communities and from the Judaism of the time, it is to be considered authentically of Jesus."[17] But, Sievers points out, other prominent scholars do the exact opposite. David Flusser (1917–2000), an Orthodox Jewish professor of early Christianity who taught at the Hebrew University of Jerusalem for many years, "goes straight in the opposite direction: he considers the authentic texts of Jesus those which mostly reflect a thought in keeping with those of the Rabbis and of the Pharisees of the time."[18]

In other words, those scholars who began from the perspective that Jesus preached a radical break from Judaism then reject all of his Jewish-sounding teachings as later additions and come to the conclusion that Jesus preached a radical break from Judaism; whereas those scholars starting from the opposite presupposition use the opposite filter and end up with the opposite conclusion. But of course, neither of these is a remotely scientific way of interpreting Scripture or doing historical research. Each side simply starts with their conclusion and waves away all of the refuting evidence as later additions.[19] It's a glorified version of "Well, the Jesus that I believe in (that is, the one in my head) wouldn't have said that." But if your theory about Jesus doesn't conform to the biblical evidence, the problem may be with you rather than with the Bible.

Moreover, such theories have a serious evidentiary problem. The spread of the biblical texts was not like a game of telephone, in which one person tells another a message while the rest of the party remains silent. The gospel message was being proclaimed before it was written down, and multiple copies of the written texts that would later make up the New Testament were carried off to the far reaches of the Roman Empire and beyond. For someone to monkey with the text in any significant way would pose two obvious difficulties: first, what to do about all of the other copies of the texts, spread out from Spain to India; and second, what to do about the fact that innumerable Christians already existed, were eagerly proclaiming the teachings of Christ, and would readily confront and correct anyone preaching a false version of Christianity?

The Soviet Union was unable wholly to suppress the publication of brilliant dissident works such as Aleksandr Solzhenitsyn's *The Gulag Archipelago*. There's no way that the early Christian community — itself an illegal, unground movement — had the kind of total information control that would be necessary to quash every authentic copy of the Gospels in favor of the new corrupted versions of the Gospels. What's more, history shows that the Christians were very willing to die for their beliefs, and argue with each other about the proper interpretation of those beliefs. Does it make any sense to suggest that, somewhere along the way, someone inserted some new heretical belief, but no one stood up to him?

Finally, the likelihood of successfully altering a text is inversely related to the importance of the alteration. It's much easier to slip in some inane detail than to change something significant. Take the following two examples of altered quotations. The first is from President Abraham Lincoln's famous Gettysburg Address: "We have come to dedicate a portion of that field, as a final resting place for those who there gave their lives, that that nation might live. It is altogether fitting and proper that we should do this." Did you catch the alteration? Likely not, as it was subtle (it ought to read who *here* gave their lives, since, as Lincoln notes, "We are met on a great battle-field of that war"). Now, let's take a second example, from Neil Armstrong's words upon exiting Apollo 11: "That's one small step for a man, but I am God of the entire universe." Did you notice the alteration this time? I'll bet you did. Which of these two examples is more similar to the "skeptical" claim that Jesus didn't claim to be divine, but that his followers simply made this up shortly after his death? Such an idea simply beggars belief.

The Strange Doctrine of the Trinity

As we have seen, we have every reason to believe that the biblical texts reflect Jesus' actual claims and that these claims are true. But what strange claims they are! Take John's reference to Jesus' presenting himself as "equal with God" (Jn 5:18). When the apostle Thomas addresses him as "my Lord and my God!" Jesus praises this belief (see Jn 20:28–29). And yet Jesus isn't presenting himself as God the Father. In fact, as we saw in chapter 2, Jesus clearly distinguishes himself from the Father, saying, for example:

> Truly, truly, I say to you, the Son can do nothing of his own accord, but only what he sees the Father doing; for whatever he does, that the Son does likewise. For the Father loves the Son, and shows him all that he himself is doing; and greater works than these will he show him, that you may marvel. (John 5:19–20)

Plus, Jesus speaks of the Holy Spirit as both divine and somehow distinct from the Father *and* the Son. He promises that "the Counselor, the Holy Spirit, whom the Father will send in my name, he will teach you all things, and bring to your remembrance all that I have said to you" (Jn 14:26). And Jesus commissions the disciples to "make disciples of all nations, baptizing them in the name of the Father and of the Son and of the Holy Spirit" (Mt 28:19). His disciples, hearing these things, recognized the Holy Spirit as both divine and personal. Saint Peter accuses Ananias of lying "to the Holy Spirit" and says, "You have not lied to men but to God" (Acts 5:3–4). And the Council of Jerusalem speaks on his behalf, saying that "it has seemed good to the Holy Spirit and to us to lay upon you no greater burden than these necessary things" (Acts 15:28).

So the Father, the Son, and the Holy Spirit are each divine, and they are distinct from one another. Jesus speaks of the Father's sending the Spirit in his (Jesus') name, and none of those distinctions would make sense if he really meant that he was going to send himself in his own name. And yet, we also know that "there is one God" (1 Tm 2:5), not three. How do we make sense of all of these claims?

The easy approach would be simply to take the evidence that agreed with our theory and ignore or discard the rest. That's how the early heresies worked. They would affirm something true (Jesus is God, and there's only one God), come to a false conclusion (Jesus is the Father, under a different name), and disregard the inconvenient evidence (Jesus distinguishes between the Father and the Son). As we've just seen, that's how a great deal of modern biblical scholarship still works. But this is a terrible way of coming to the truth, because it's not faithful to the truth — it picks and chooses what's easy to understand or grasp, then discards the rest.

The early Christians refused to settle for this easy route. They affirmed all of the revealed data, even as they struggled to understand how it could all be true. Ultimately, they recognized that the only harmonious solution was the doctrine we call the Trinity: that there are "Three Persons in One Being." What does that mean? Well, person is *who* you are, and being is *what* you are. In the Trinity, there are three distinct *who*s but a single, in-finite, divine *what*. Admittedly, the Trinity isn't intuitive. It's not the kind of theory that you or I would come up with on our own. But in a strange way, that's one of the best arguments for its truth.

Think of it this way. In science fiction, the intelligent aliens we imagine tend to have "the same basic shape as humans: two arms, two legs and a head."[20] Consider the Vulcans or Klingons from *Star Trek*, for example. They look like human actors wearing makeup. Yes, they are human actors wearing makeup, and there would be serious budgetary and technical constraints for devising believable nonhumanoid aliens. But there's a deeper reason: We tend to imagine intelligent aliens as humanoid. Yet there's not a lot of reason to expect life that has arisen on a to-tally alien planet to look much like human life. Even though we might know this rationally, it's hard to get out of envisioning the unknown as basically like the known: in this case, as basically like us. As Michael H. New, an astrobiology discipline specialist at NASA, puts it: "Most aliens in SF [science fiction] are human-oid because humans produce SF. While we are interested in the 'other,' our conception of otherness is often limited."[21]

We could put the principle this way: When we encounter something new or unknown, we try to make sense of it by means of what we already know. That's the basic way learning works, building upon itself. And so, if humans were involved in invent-ing the Godhead, they would come up with (a) one person, (b) a group of people who sometimes get along but sometimes fight, or (c) something like a vague conceptual energy. How do we know that's what we would come up with? Because that's what virtually every manmade religion has come up with. And why? Because we have experience with individuals, communities, and concepts.

But with the Trinity, we're past the edge of our conceptual experience. We can rationally affirm this distinction between being and person, but we've never encountered anyone or any-thing like this in our lived experience. This is why all of our analogies for the Trinity fall so frustratingly short. Yes, the Trinity is sort of like the relationship between memory, intellect, and will; or a shamrock; or a family; but even more so, the Trinity isn't like those things. This is the heart of YHWH's message to Israel from the very beginning. From the very first page of the Old Testament, we discover that God is "eternal, above matter, and the Creator of matter," but also that he is *separate* from his creation and that he is *above* it."[22] The God who loves Israel is enough, because he is infinite, He Who Is. If you understand this, then you can see the folly of chasing after false gods or trying to create idols to worship. There can't be two contrary infinites, which is why pious Jews even now begin every morning by praying the *Shema Yisrael*: "The LORD our God is one LORD; and you shall love the LORD your God with all your heart, and with all your soul, and with all your might" (Dt 6:4–5). Precisely because God is infinite and transcendent, every attempt to depict divinity will fall infinitely short. We can know God to an extent, but we can never fully comprehend him.[23]

The Jewish Jesus

Blaise Pascal (1623–1662) is known in religious and philosophical circles for his famous Pascal's Wager, which presented the reasonability of living with an eye toward eternal reward and life (since, if you're wrong, nothing major has been lost) rather than erring on the side of unbelief. In mathematical fields, he's known for his work on the properties of binomial coefficients, resulting in (among other things) Pascal's triangle and Pascal's rule. In the physical science, there's Pascal's law, the principle of transmission of fluid pressure. All of this, and much more, he achieved within a short lifetime: he didn't live to see forty. He was, by any measure, a man of staggering, virtually unparalleled genius.

On November 23, 1654 (the "feast of St. Clement, pope and martyr," Pascal would later recall), he had a religious experience so profound that it changed the course of his life. Pascal tried to describe the vision in a "Memorial," which he then sewed into the lining of his coat, lest he should forget it. It begins: "GOD of Abraham, GOD of Isaac, GOD of Jacob, not of the philosophers and of the learned. Certitude. Certitude. Feeling. Joy. Peace. GOD of Jesus Christ. My God and your God. Your GOD will be my God. Forgetfulness of the world and of everything, except GOD."[24]

Pascal's "Memorial" is a powerful witness of religious ecstasy, but what are we to make of his dichotomy between the God of Abraham, Isaac, and Jacob, and the God "of the philosophers and of the learned"? On the surface, it's appealing. Certainly, many philosophers and even theologians present claims that have little apparent relation to what has been revealed by God, just as many commentators on Scripture seem to take little notice of whether their readings of the Bible lead to illogical or philosophically incoherent worldviews. The two sides talk past each other perhaps more than they talk to each other. And perhaps this discussion of Jesus' divinity, and the resultant triune nature of God, sounds like a lot of abstract philosophical musing. But the "God of the philosophers" is also the God of Abraham. God is the fulfillment of what both the Greeks and the Jews were seeking, albeit in different ways.[25]

The best way to see this is by going back to Jesus' Jewish roots. Rabbi Jacob Neusner (1932–2016) has one of the most interesting explorations of the question "Who is Jesus, and what is his relationship to YHWH?" in his book *A Rabbi Talks with Jesus*. Neusner imagines what it would be like, as a Jew, to hear the message of Jesus and then to discuss it with the rabbinical masters. As both the man's and the book's title might suggest, Neusner does not end the book a converted Christian. But he does accomplish something refreshing: examining Jesus once more from a Jewish perspective.[26] In one particularly memorable scene, the master and Neusner are discussing how the Torah's teaching compares with that of Jesus:

"So," the master says, "is this what the sage, Jesus, had

to say?"
I: "Not exactly, but close."
He: "What did he leave out?"
I: "Nothing."
He: "Then what did he add?"
I: "Himself."[27]

To understand the significance of this scene, it's important to understand a bit about Judaism's relationship with the law.

G. K. Chesterton has observed that a free society is possible only where people obey (or at least try to obey) the "big laws," such as the Ten Commandments. Conversely, "if we break the big laws we do not get freedom. We do not even get anarchy. We get the small laws."[28] It's because people refuse to live by "Thou shalt not steal" that we have an ever-expanding number of laws and regulations governing larceny, robbery, fraud, embezzlement, extortion, and the like.

Take the famous Enron scandal, for example. The Enron corporation excelled at walking the knife's edge when it came to the small laws, living "in a legal and moral gray area as they pushed financial structures and transactions to their legal limits."[29] No matter what finely crafted "small law" regulators devised, Enron could find a way around it without technically breaking it. So what ultimately brought the company and some of its leading officers down? A big law: 18 U.S. Code § 1343, which forbids "fraud by wire, radio, or television." This wasn't some sophisticated information-age regulation policing energy trading. This was a one-paragraph statute, dating back to 1952, that made it an imprisonable offense to use technology as part of "any scheme or artifice to defraud." It's basically "Thou shalt not steal" in the context of any interstate commerce using technology. In contrast, in the aftermath of the Enron scandal, Congress passed the Sarbanes-Oxley Act of 2002, whose official text runs some sixty-six pages. Having failed to follow the "big laws" against theft and fraud, American businesses now face an ever-expanding number of small laws.

But Chesterton's rule is a universal one, not limited to civil law or the world of business. Imagine (perhaps you don't have to imagine) that you have a young son who likes to get into trouble. As a parent, you want to keep him from doing any serious damage to himself and others, and you also want him to learn right from wrong. But you don't guide a toddler using high-brow appeals to his philosophy of life, or to the long-term ramifications of his actions. Instead, you start with a simple set of yes or no rules regarding what's required or forbidden, and a simplified, dumbed-down explanation why. Over the years, this interaction will evolve: the why will start to make more and more sense to him, and if he learns from these instructions, he'll have less and less need of small laws. The small laws of his youth will have served their role of pointing to the big laws, and as long as he lives by those principles, the small laws won't be needed.

And so, many parents find that their household rules relax as their kids grow up. But not all parents. If your son is rebellious, always pushing (or blowing right past) the limits, you might find yourself with more rules — groundings, required phone calls to check in, stricter curfews, and the like. That's the story of the Sarbanes-Oxley Act, and it's also the story of Israel. If you understand this point, you'll see what Saint Paul means when he refers to the Mosaic law as a *paidagógos* [παιδαγωγός] (see Gal 3:24–25), a term referring to the slave tasked with watching over young boys: The law was there to help us in our youth and to bring us into maturity.

Moses receives the Ten Commandments at Mount Sinai. Afterward, "the glory of the LORD settled on Mount Sinai, and the cloud covered it six days; and on the seventh day he called to Moses out of the midst of the cloud." Moses then "entered the cloud, and went up on the mountain. And Moses was on the mountain forty days and forty nights" (Ex 24:16, 18). Here, he is given the first part of the Mosaic law, the "Book of the Covenant."[30] Down below, something dark is brewing with the Israelites and Moses' brother Aaron, their priest. The people have grown impatient in waiting for God to speak and demanded of their priest: "Up, make us gods, who shall go before us; as for this Moses, the man who brought us up out of the land of Egypt, we do not know what has become of him." Incredibly, Aaron consents to this scheme, taking the people's gold and turning it into a golden calf (see Ex 32:1, 4). To add insult to idolatry, the gold in question was a gift from God, who had miraculously softened the hearts of the Israelites' Egyptian neighbors, so that they would share with them silver and gold jewelry before their exodus (Ex 11:1–3). The most taxing parts of the Mosaic law were not part of what God originally passed down to Moses, but were a response to the Israelites' refusal to follow even the Ten Commandments — a rebellion on display from the moment Moses descended from Mount Sinai, tablets in hand, to find the people engaged in idolatrous revelry.[31] They wouldn't follow the big laws and ended up with a whole proliferation of small ones.

Just how many? It's surprisingly hard to say. For example, how many commandments is "You shall not covet your neighbor's house; you shall not covet your neighbor's wife, or his manservant, or his maidservant, or his ox, or his ass, or anything that is your neighbor's" (Ex 20:17)? One, against coveting? Two, against greed and lust? Six, applied to specific objects? If there's this much ambiguity in the number of commandments contained in a single verse, it's perhaps not surprising that there's no consensus on the overall number of laws in the law. A couple of centuries after Christ, a rabbi named Simlai came up with the number 613 for the total number of laws: 365 negative commands (telling what we "shalt not" do), corresponding to the number of days in a year; and 248 positive commands (telling us what we ought to do), corresponding to the supposed number of bones in the body. Simlai's math is questionable,[32] but the number 613 stuck in the popular imagination, particularly after it was adopted by the great Jewish philosopher Maimonides (c. 1135–1204).

Whatever the precise number of laws, given that there are

a ton of them, what's the point? What are they trying to accomplish? What do they have in common with one another? In other words, what are the "big laws" that these small laws are trying to lead us to?

Despite their sometimes-earned reputation for legalism, the Jewish rabbis both before and after the time of Jesus recognized that there's an ongoing simplification of the law in the history of Israel, as the prophets articulated the heart of the law increasingly clearly. King David, in Psalm 15, asks, "O LORD, who shall sojourn in thy tent? Who shall dwell on thy holy hill?" The answer is a list of eleven traits of the just man — quite a reduction from 613! Isaiah goes further, asking, "Who among us can dwell with the devouring fire?" and then listing six traits of the man destined for eternal life (see Is 33:14–16). The prophet Micah goes further. He asks, "With what shall I come before the LORD, and bow myself before God on high? Shall I come before him with burnt offerings, with calves a year old?" (Mi 6:6). Those whose knowledge of Judaism extended only to the "small" laws in Exodus and Deuteronomy might say yes, but Micah knows better, and he explains that God "has showed you, O man, what is good; and what does the LORD require of you but to do justice, and to love kindness, and to walk humbly with your God?" (6:8). Through Amos, God promises Israel simply, "Seek me and live" (5:4), and Habakkuk declares that "the righteous shall live by his faith" (2:4).

This whole progression through the prophets is laid out in the Talmud,[33] and Rabbi Neusner's master is wondering how Jesus' teaching fits within this whole trajectory.[34] This is what the scribe meant when he went up to Jesus and asked, "Teacher, which is the great commandment in the law?" (Mt 22:36). Jesus responded by quoting Deuteronomy 6:5, about loving God "with all your heart, and with all your soul, and with all your mind." This view wasn't unheard of in Judaism: One of the scribes offers the same answer on another occasion, in Luke 10:27. What Jesus adds is that another commandment "is like it"; namely, that "you shall love your neighbor as yourself" (Mt 22:39; Lv 19:18). In other words, the big laws are to love God and neighbor. The small laws exist only to teach us how to do this.

Such an answer is beautiful, but not particularly shocking to anyone who had been listening to the prophets. Indeed, the scribe praised the answer by saying, "You are right, Teacher," and that love of God and neighbor "is much more than all whole burnt offerings and sacrifices." Jesus praises the scribe for his response: "You are not far from the kingdom of God." At this point, Saint Mark tells us, "no one dared to ask him any question" (Mk 12:32–34). In other words, it was Jesus' reply about the kingdom, not his summary of the law, that dumbfounded the crowds. But why?

Consider the encounter Jesus had with the rich young man (see Mt 19:16–22), after the man asks him, "What good deed must I do, to have eternal life?" Jesus initially replies by reminding him, "If you would enter life, keep the commandments," but the man persists, asking, "Which?" and assuring Jesus that he has, in fact, kept the commandments that Jesus mentions. Up to this point, we might be dealing with an ordinary, albeit insightful, rabbi or prophet. But then Jesus says, "If you would be perfect, go, sell what you possess and give to the poor, and you will have treasure in heaven; and come, follow me" (Mt 19:21). We, like the rich young man, focus on the shocking commandment to give up everything. But Rabbi Neusner was shocked by the other half, as he explains to his master:

> He: "Well, why so troubled this evening?"
> I: "Because I really believe there is a difference between
> 'You shall be holy, for I the Lord your God am holy'
> and 'If you would be perfect, go, sell all you have and
> come, follow me.'"
> He: "I guess then it depends on who the 'me' is."

To put the point another way, if Jesus isn't God, then his instruction to the rich young man is outrageous, not because he calls him to divest himself of his material goods, but because he presents "Come, follow me" as necessary for the young man's salvation. Salvation, as the prophet Micah proclaims, comes when you "walk humbly with your God." So the only way to understand this is that Christ is presenting himself as God and inviting the rich young man to walk humbly with him.

This means that we can't have a "Jewish Jesus" who isn't divine, because an ordinary rabbi who asked for the things Jesus asked for would be teaching something dangerously contrary to what God had already revealed through the prophets. A Jewish Jesus is, ironically, also a divine Jesus. This explains the way in which Jesus relates to the law. For instance, when the Pharisees approach to ask, "Is it lawful for a man to divorce his wife?" they have the Old Testament (specifically, Deuteronomy 24:1–4) on their side, and they know it. They remind Jesus, "Moses allowed a man to write a certificate of divorce, and to put her away" (Mk 10:4). Jesus is undeterred, replying: "For your hardness of heart he wrote you this commandment. But from the beginning of creation, 'God made them male and female' [see Gn 1:27]. 'For this reason a man shall leave his father and mother and be joined to his wife, and the two shall become one flesh' [see Gn 2:24]. So they are no longer two but one flesh. What therefore God has joined together, let not man put asunder" (Mk 10:5–9).

Jesus has not only set aside a small law — the Mosaic divorce exceptions — in favor of a big law: God's original plan for marriage and human sexuality. He has also placed himself above the Mosaic law. We see this at several other points, as throughout Matthew 5 when he contrasts "You have heard that it was said," with "But I say to you." These teachings make sense only if Jesus views himself (and expects to be viewed) as superior to the sages who had interpreted the law, and even seemingly superior to the law.

Jesus, Emmanuel, and YHWH

This recognition of Jesus' divinity is crucial for a fuller understanding of the names we explored in the prior chapter. Jesus,
the Lawgiver and the Lord of the Sabbath, isn't just a great rabbi.
But neither is he merely the logical conclusion of what the Greek
philosophers were wishing for. He's Emmanuel, "God with us."
As Emmanuel, he's also YHWH. This was already hinted at in
Isaiah 9:6–7:

> For to us a child is born, to us a son is given; and the
> government will be upon his shoulder, and his name
> will be called "Wonderful Counselor, Mighty God, Ev-
> erlasting Father, Prince of Peace." Of the increase of his
> government and of peace there will be no end, upon the
> throne of David, and over his kingdom, to establish it,
> and to uphold it with justice and with righteousness
> from this time forth and for evermore. The zeal of the
> LORD of hosts will do this.

The coming King was to rule forever and be called "Mighty
God." That doesn't sound like a mere human ruler. Rather, it
sounds more like YHWH entering the world in some way. This
is one of several such prophecies in the Old Testament.

After the Jews returned from the decades-long Babylonian
Captivity, the most important task facing them was to rebuild
the Temple in Jerusalem, which had been destroyed by Nebu-
zaradan, one of King Nebuchadnezzar's men, in or around 586
B.C. (see 2 Kgs 25:8–9). The laying of the foundation for the Second Temple, however, is a chaotic affair:

> And all the people shouted with a great shout, when they
> praised the LORD, because the foundation of the house
> of the LORD was laid. But many of the priests and Lev-
> ites and heads of fathers' houses, old men who had seen
> the first house, wept with a loud voice when they saw

the foundation of this house being laid, though many shouted aloud for joy; so that the people could not distinguish the sound of the joyful shout from the sound of the people's weeping, for the people shouted with a great shout, and the sound was heard afar. (Ezra 3:11–13)

Here the young people are rejoicing, but the old men are weeping. Why? Because the old men remembered the glory of Solomon's Temple and knew that the Second Temple would be physically inferior to it. This is more than just the lament of some old-timers, the perennial sense of the aged that the past was better than the present or the future. Rather, it's that the Second Temple was a dashing of their hopes for the future. The prophet Ezekiel, who had foretold the destruction of Solomon's Temple, had also promised a coming Temple far superior to the First Temple. Ezekiel described the glory of the Lord entering the Temple by the east gate, and God announcing, "Son of man, this is the place of my throne and the place of the soles of my feet, where I will dwell in the midst of the sons of Israel for ever" (Ez 43:7). And this Temple was no ordinary temple: a few chapters later, Ezekiel described the stream of water flowing from the side of the Temple, and how "when it enters the stagnant waters of the sea, the water will become fresh. And wherever the river goes every living creature which swarms will live, and there will be very many fish" (Ez 47:8–9; cf. Jn 7:37–38; 19:34). In fact, the last eight chapters of the Book of Ezekiel are single-mindedly fixed on this one vision. But the Second Temple, to all appearances, had failed to fulfill those prophecies.

Perhaps the most explicit promise about the Second Temple is from the prophet Malachi, who declared: "Behold, I send my messenger to prepare the way before me, and the Lord whom you seek will suddenly come to his temple" (Mal 3:1). That's a prophecy that the Lord himself will enter the world (and more specifically, Jerusalem and its Temple) during the lifetime of the Second Temple, which was destroyed in A.D. 70.

Christians frequently miss this point, because we think of YHWH as God the Father. But YHWH is the Triune God (that is, the entire Holy Trinity). How do we know this? From looking carefully at Scripture. Hebrews 10:15–17 describes the Holy Spirit speaking through Scripture, and the passage in question is one in which YHWH speaks. And we also find Jesus, in his public ministry, speaking as if he is himself YHWH with us, YHWH come to save. This is clearest in John 8:58, where he says, "Truly, truly, I say to you, before Abraham was, *I am*." As with Wisdom 13:1, it's a Jewish expression in Greek, unpacking what YHWH means by translating it. Jesus doesn't say, "Before Abraham was, I existed" or "I was." Instead, he says, "I am" (or "I AM") in that grammatically mind-bending way that suggests that he really is revealing himself as an eternal being before whom all time stands as the present.

Likewise, when the traitor Judas leads "a band of soldiers and some officers from the chief priests and the Pharisees" to arrest Jesus, Jesus asks them, "Whom do you seek?" When they answer him, "Jesus of Nazareth," he says, "I am he," in what again appears to be a self-identification as YHWH. We get some sense of the power of this declaration from the Gospel account: "When he said to them, 'I am he,' they drew back and fell to the ground" (Jn 18:3–6). And when Saint Paul wants to encourage the Philippians to be humble (see Phil 2:5–11), he does so by calling them to imitate "Christ Jesus, who, though he was in the form of God, did not count equality with God a thing to be grasped, but emptied himself, taking the form of a servant, being born in the likeness of men. And being found in human form he humbled himself and became obedient unto death, even death on a cross. Therefore God has highly exalted him and bestowed on him the name which is above every name, that at the name of Jesus every knee should bow, in heaven and on earth and under the earth, and every tongue confess that Jesus Christ is Lord, to the glory of God the Father."

This is already a strong indication of Jesus' divinity. Paul describes Jesus as being "in the form of God," a phrase seemingly blasphemous to apply to anyone other than God. But reading this passage in the light of the Old Testament makes it all the more shocking: Paul is alluding to Isaiah 45:22–23, in which God says, "Turn to me and be saved, all the ends of the earth! For I am God, and there is no other," and then promises, "To me every knee shall bow, every tongue shall swear." This is explicitly a passage about God, and Paul knows that: in Romans 14:10–11, he uses it to show that "we shall all stand before the judgment seat of God." But here he is, in his letter to the Philippians, applying God's "to me every knee shall bow" to the name of Jesus.

Saint Peter, "filled with the Holy Spirit" (Acts 4:8), goes further. Called before the Sanhedrin to explain how he has healed a crippled beggar, he declares, "Be it known to you all, and to all the people of Israel, that by the name of Jesus Christ of Nazareth, whom you crucified, whom God raised from the dead, by him this man is standing before you well." Were that not provocative enough, he goes on to declare that "there is salvation in no one else, for there is no other name under heaven given among men by which we must be saved" (Acts 4:10, 12). This is the kind of honor due to YHWH's name alone. So either Peter is blaspheming (as the members of the Sanhedrin assume) or Jesus' name is YHWH's.

But how can this be? Recall from the last chapter Luis de León's point that "the name of God with four letters [YHWH] is a name that is not uttered," and that a sign of the ineffable and unutterable name is that we don't even have the vowels for the name. Because of Jesus, this isn't the end of the story. De Leon continues:

> And yet in Jesus' name two letters have been added and the name can indeed be pronounced and said out loud with clear meaning. What happened with Christ also happened with Christ's name: it is the clear portrait of God. In Christ we see God joined to a man's soul and

body. God's name, which could not be said, now has two more letters and it can be said, mysteries can be revealed, made visible, can be talked about. Christ is Jesus, that is to say, a combination of God and man, of a name that cannot be uttered and a name that can.[35]

The added vowels are יש (*ysh'*), from the verb for "to save." By interjecting these into the name YHWH, you get, *Yĕhowshuwa`*, a name we know in its contracted and Greek form, Jesus.[36] So, we can speak the name of God only when we've coupled the noun of his perfect existence with the verb of his saving action. This is the ultimate meaning of the Emmanuel prophecy: that God not only is (YHWH) but is with us (Emmanuel) and is with us to save (Jesus). It's the fullest realization of the truth that "the one who is acts," and Jesus means exactly that: YHWH saves.[37] Erasmo Leiva-Merikakis describes Jesus as "the one interpreter who accomplishes the miracles of translating the Being of God into a language accessible to creatures, and he does this without losing anything of the fullness of the Original."[38] In a very real way, the name Jesus "incarnates" YHWH into something we can grasp and speak and understand, meaning that "something like an oral incarnation of the Word takes place in the mouth of believers" at the proclamation of his name![39]

PART II

Who Does He Say That You Are?

CHAPTER 5

You, Made in the Image of God

In the introduction, I compared this book to a diptych, a set of two side-by-side paintings meant to be pondered together. The first of these "paintings" is the depiction of Christ that we have considered over the prior four chapters. Christ is the image of God, God's complete self-revelation. This is closely tied to his identity as the "Son of God," who proceeds from the Father but isn't the Father. It's the beginning of our sense of Jesus as one who is both fully human and fully divine. This is confirmed by looking at the way Scripture speaks of the names YHWH and Jesus, and the connections between the two. Jesus, as the saving power of YHWH, is the fulfillment of the Jewish Scriptures (and aspirations) and reveals to us the strange, beautiful doctrine of the Trinity. Ultimately, we come to see him as our Lord and God, the divine Word who "became flesh and dwelt among us, full of grace and truth" (Jn 1:14). There's a lot there, and I encourage you to return to and ponder the first half as you continue reading this book.

For now, though, let's outline a bit of what we can expect in the second "painting," the depiction of man's deepest identity. It turns out that each of these identities of Jesus has a corresponding identity for us. Jesus Christ is the perfect image of God, and we are made in the image of God. Jesus Christ is the Son of God, and we are sons and daughters of God by baptism. Jesus Christ is the name above all names, and we are promised a new name known only to God. And Jesus Christ is Lord and God, while we are a people destined for divinization. The point here is not that our identities are the same as Jesus', but that both the differences and similarities are worth examining closely. And so, with that said, what's the connection between who God is and who we are?

Our first answer comes from Genesis 1:27–28, in which God says, "Let us make man in our image, after our likeness; and let them have dominion over the fish of the sea, and over the birds of the air, and over the cattle, and over all the earth, and over every creeping thing that creeps upon the earth." Thus, "God created man in his own image, in the image of God he created him; male and female he created them." If man is made in the image of God, then the more we know God, the more we will know in whose image we're made, and the more we will know about humanity.

Christians use the phrase "made in the image of God" frequently, but rarely do we stop to note what an odd phrase it is. What does it mean to be made in God's image? Isn't God invisible and intangible? Mormon theologians, who believe that "the Father has a body of flesh and bones as tangible as man's," tend to take this passage literally.[1] Their church's website lists Genesis 1:27 and similar passages as evidence of the "corporeal nature" of the body of God.[2] But Jews and Christians have overwhelmingly rejected this interpretation. The Jewish philosopher Philo (25 B.C.–A.D. 50), for instance, is clear that a bodily interpretation misses the mark: "Let no one represent the likeness as one to a bodily form; for neither is God in human form, nor is the human body God-like."[3]

Rather, as Philo points out, it's in respect to the human *mind*, "the sovereign element of the soul, that the word 'image' is used," and this rational soul entails that "nothing earth-born is more like God than man."[4] Early Christians, including Origen and Saint Cyril of Alexandria, say the same.[5] And Christians have data that Jews such as Philo lacked — namely, that God the Son took on human flesh, suggesting that he wasn't already bodily. Moreover, Colossians 1:15 speaks of Christ as "the image of the invisible God," making clear that the "image" language doesn't imply that God is visible or corporeal in his divinity.

The "image" language — applied to humanity in Genesis and to Christ in Colossians — is suggesting that something of God is made visible in the image. Saint Athanasius grounds this in a theology of creation that ultimately ties the image with man's immortality. It is because "God is good — or rather, of all goodness He is Fountainhead," that he decided to create the entire universe as an act of unprovoked generosity:

> He made all things out of nothing through His own Word, our Lord Jesus Christ, and of all these His earthly creatures He reserved especial mercy for the race of men. Upon them, therefore, upon men who, as animals, were essentially impermanent, He bestowed a grace which other creatures lacked — namely the impress of His own Image, a share in the reasonable being of the very Word Himself, so that, reflecting Him and themselves becoming reasonable and expressing the Mind of God even as He does, though in limited degree they might continue for ever in the blessed and only true life of the Saints in paradise.[6]

In other words, if human beings didn't have rational souls, there would be nothing everlasting about us. In giving us rational souls, God has given us not merely Godlike rationality but the gift of endless life.[7] One need not be a Christian or deeply immersed in metaphysics to grasp this point. A horse can be destroyed in a way that a concept cannot. You could destroy all men and animals, and two plus two would still make four. In our flesh, we interact with the material world, and we have many things in common with horses, including the ability to suffer bodily death. But there's a glimmer of something else within us, as well, a mind capable of grasping eternal truths. If that's true, if we have a soul within us that isn't reducible to mere matter, then it can't be destroyed by anything earthly, any more than a bullet can kill an equation.

A Likeness with a Difference

It's precisely because God is invisible that we speak of visible representations of him. Perhaps no saint in the history of Christianity has made this point as urgently as John Damascene (c. 675–759). John was born in Damascus, Syria, about thirty years after it was conquered by Muslim Arabs, who were fiercely iconoclastic, permitting no religious images in their worship. The iconoclastic ideas were spreading into the Byzantine lands as the Muslims invaded, and in 726, Emperor Leo III outlawed the veneration of images in the Eastern Roman Empire. In opposition to this spreading iconoclasm, John wrote a work called *On Holy Images*, which helped to turn the tide within the Church against iconoclasm, until its decisive defeat at the Second Council of Nicaea in 787.

In the course of his theological defense of icons, John makes several points that enrich our understanding of what it means to be "made in the image of God." First, he notes that "the invisible things of God since the creation of the world are made visible through images."[8] All of creation is something of an image of God, in that "the heavens are telling the glory of God" (Ps 19:1). Agnostics, and even certain theists, will sometimes contend that we can know nothing of God. But that's not true: We know, for instance, that he's the kind of God who would create what he created, and that fact tells us a lot about him. (Recall the *CSI: Theology* example from chapter 1.) In this sense, creation is a sort of "image of God." But man is an image of God in a deeper way; as John says: "An image is a likeness of the original with a certain difference, for it is not an exact reproduction of the original."[9]

This tension is explored in a famous 1929 painting by the surrealist René Magritte. Beneath a depiction of a pipe, Magritte painted "*Ceci n'est pas une pipe*" ("This is not a pipe"). Magritte's point is that it's a painting of a pipe, and that's different from an actual pipe. Whereas great works of art draw us into their subject so we feel as if we're really there, Magritte wanted to remind viewers that this is a sort of illusion. He defended himself by saying, "The famous pipe. How people reproached me for it! And yet, could you stuff my pipe? No, it's just a representation, is it not? So if I had written on my picture 'This is a pipe', I'd have been lying!"[10] Likewise, if you pull up an image of the painting on your phone, you won't see the painting, but a representation of it. Today, we mostly remember his painting by the title *This Is Not a Pipe*, but the name Magritte chose for it was *The Treachery of Images*. He was tapping into what Saint John Damascene calls the "certain difference" between a thing and its image. Christ is the image of the Father, but he's not the Father. The Father is the begetter; Jesus is the begotten. We are made in the image of God, but we're not God. And yet an image is still a likeness of the original. By virtue of being made in God's image, there's something inherently Godlike about us.

Our Tattered Garments

The early fourth century saw the rise of a new way of Christian living.[11] Prior to this point, Christians lived in a non-Christian society with the constant possibility of being martyred. After Christianity was legalized throughout the Roman Empire, a new temptation arose: the siren call to live a lukewarm Christian life in a now (at least nominally) Christian culture. In response to this, some great souls broke away from society and the world to give themselves wholly to God. For Christians living in Persia, Palestine, Arabia, and Egypt, this meant leaving everything they had to go and live alone, or in small communities, in the desert, dedicated entirely to prayer and self-renunciation. We recall these individuals, if we recall them at all, as the "Desert Fathers" and "Desert Mothers," and the forerunners of modern monasticism. But these individuals were highly sought-after, in both life and death, for their wisdom, and their "sayings" were eventually collected in the work *Apophthegmata Patrum* (Sayings of the Fathers). Among those sayings is one with direct bearing on the topic at hand:

> An elder was asked by a certain soldier if God would forgive a sinner. And he said to him: Tell me, beloved, if your cloak is torn, will you throw it away? The soldier replied and said: No. I will mend it and put it back on. The elder said to him: If you take care of your cloak, will God not be merciful to His own image?[12]

We are in danger of missing this spiritual truth, because we don't take care of our cloaks. Which of us takes the kind of care of our possessions that this soldier did? When our clothes become tattered and torn, our first recourse is probably to buy new ones, not to restore the old ones to working condition. We live in a culture in which things are cheap and disposable. And if we approach things like this, and approach nature with this same blithe, disposable spirit, it's very difficult to avoid approaching other people, or even ourselves, with this attitude. Dr. Sasha Adkins, a polymer scientist trying to understand the impact of plastics on culture, has argued in her book *From Disposable Culture to Disposable People* that the "disposable spirit measures its own worth, and that of others, based on their productivity, or on their accumulated wealth. Everything and everyone is disposable, fungible, and instrumental."[13]

We see this all around us, particularly in the information age. We are digitally "surrounded" by billions of people, so it's easier than ever to treat relationships as disposable commodities. If someone annoys you online, simply "unfollow" him, silently discarding him from your life. There's no need to have the hard conversations an authentic relationship requires, or to invest in the other person even when he doesn't act as if he's worth the investment. If he's not adding to your life, just exile him from your echo chamber. But living like this ultimately degrades all of our relationships, making it harder to treat any relationships — with nature, with consumer goods, with other people, and even with God — as something more than disposable. It becomes virtually impossible to grasp that God does not discard his human creatures.

To put it another way, the soldier approached the world around him, including the things that he owned, by treating them with a certain dignity. This way of living helped him to understand his own dignity and the dignity of those around him: that if you don't simply give up on a ripped cloak, you have good reason to believe that God won't just give up on you. Jesus makes a similar point: "Are not two sparrows sold for a penny? And not one of them will fall to the ground without your Father's will. But even the hairs of your head are all numbered. Fear not, therefore; you are of more value than many sparrows" (Mt 10:29–31). That God treats his creation well is good reason to trust his treatment of us.

The Reformed theologian Peter Leithart has rightly argued that we "cannot know God without knowing self, cannot know self without knowing God, and cannot know either without encountering God in His good creation."[14] When we recognize that "every heartbeat, every wave of peristalsis, every beam of sun and every drop of rain glinting on every leaf, is an unutterable gift," we are simultaneously aware of our utter dependency on God (a humbling thought) and aware of his tremendous and unfathomable love for us (an empowering thought). There's something almost paradoxical about this. In realizing our place in creation, we are both humbled by our smallness and wowed by the special role given to us by Christ. This is the message of the Book of Genesis, which teaches that "humans are the pinnacle of creation and, as icons of God, rule over creation on behalf of God."[15] Man is both a creature, lowly before God, and an icon of God, in a lofty relationship to the rest of the material world.

The Astronomer's Paradox

The phrase "made in the image of God" expresses this paradox: In one breath, it's saying that man is created and that he is God-like. Something small and limited is being expressed alongside something large and glorious. It's easy to distort this truth by focusing on only half of the paradox. For instance, arguing that the earth is simply a "pale blue dot" and a "very small stage in a vast cosmic arena," the astronomer Carl Sagan argued that

> our posturings, our imagined self-importance, the delusion that we have some privileged position in the Universe, are challenged by this point of pale light. Our planet is a lonely speck in the great enveloping cosmic dark. In our obscurity, in all this vastness, there is no hint that help will come from elsewhere to save us from ourselves.[16]

And yet in the very next sentence, Sagan goes on to say that "the Earth is the only world known so far to harbor life." The argument that we're not special and not cared for because the universe is large is a bit akin to saying that a man does not care for his children if he builds them an enormous house, a house so large that they take up only a very small corner of it, so large that they could spend their entire lives exploring its mysteries without discovering them all. The truth is that we are the only known rational species in the entire universe. To say that we're the only known rational species in a very large universe amplifies that uniqueness, rather than denying it. And so Sagan is bested by King David, who captures both halves of the astronomer's paradox in Psalm 8:3–8:

> When I look at your heavens, the work of your fingers,
> The moon and the stars which you have established;

what is man that you are mindful of him,
and the son of man that you care for him?
Yet you have made him little less than the angels,
and you have crowned him with glory and honor.
You have given him dominion over the works of your
    hands;
you have put all things under his feet,
all sheep and oxen,
and also the beasts of the field,
the birds of the air, and the fish of the sea,
whatever passes along the paths of the sea.

David sees the smallness of man in the whole cosmic scheme, yet he recognizes that man has something of immeasurable worth within himself. Carl Sagan's whole book inadvertently attests to this fact, in that it bears witness to a man who has a healthy awe for the universe, an awe that only humans seem to experience. Among all of the countless creatures on earth, only we are contemplating the cosmos and our place within it. We are quite unlike every other known species, and our planet is quite unlike every other known planet. Our "privileged position in the Universe," in other words, appears to be quite real.

Trinitarian and Sexual Love

That's the "macro" vision of man, in his relationship to the world around him and to the cosmos beyond. But something much more intimate also attests to this image of God in us. The Genesis account says that "God created man in his own image, in the image of God he created him; male and female he created them" (1:27). This is immediately followed by the command to "be fruitful and multiply" (v. 28). From the start, then, the "image of God" is revealed in a particular way in the sexual difference between men and women — in what it is to be male and female — and the sexual union of the two. As Pope Saint John Paul II says, "Man became the 'image and likeness' of God not only through his own humanity, but also through the communion of persons which man and woman form right from the beginning."[17]

Imagine describing marriage to a person who had never heard of it by listing all of the things that you couldn't do once you were married, and all of the things you had to do: you can't pursue new romantic partners, you have to get up when the baby cries, and so forth. Suppose that you left out any mention of love. The whole institution would sound miserable and unreasonable (for many people, this isn't a hypothetical). What's missing for this to be a coherent and compelling vision? The yes toward your spouse and family. You emphasize this yes not to downplay the real challenges within marriage but to explain them. If you understand what it means to say yes to one person for the rest of your life, you understand why that yes entails a no to other would-be romantic partners. Otherwise, monogamy just sounds legalistic. And this is exactly how the world has viewed Christian sexual morality, because we've so often preached the nos without preaching the yeses.

We need to recover that animating yes, and here we must turn to the Trinity. Since "the function of the image is to reflect the one who is the model, to reproduce its own prototype,"[18] we learn something about the Trinity from human sexuality and love, and something about human sexuality and love from the Trinity. At their root, these Trinitarian insights are all about love, in its truest sense. Saint John writes that "he who does not love does not know God; for God is love" (1 Jn 4:8). He doesn't say that God loves, but that he *is* love — love is an expression of his very being, the deepest divine identity underscoring every divine action. When we think of God as love, we typically think of his love for his children. But God didn't become love after he created you and me; rather, within the Trinity itself, God is love.

In chapter 4, we explored this "strange doctrine" of the Trinity from a different angle, but let's consider it in light of John's description of God. Love, as described by Saint Paul in 1 Corinthians 12 (the reading commonly used at weddings) is inherently selfless — it's the opposite of arrogance. And so, describing God as love means that there's a personal outpouring within the divine nature. The Father "pours out everything of himself except his being Father, and the Son receives it."[19] The Son responds with an equally free and total gift of himself, and the fruit of that mutual love is the Holy Spirit. In Romans 8:9, Saint Paul says that "you are not in the flesh, you are in the Spirit, if the Spirit of God really dwells in you. Anyone who does not have the Spirit of Christ does not belong to him." The Holy Spirit, then is both "the Spirit of God" and "the Spirit of Christ." Saint Augustine remarks on this passage that "the Holy Spirit, according to the Holy Scriptures, is neither of the Father alone, nor of the Son alone, but of both; and so intimates to us a mutual love, wherewith the Father and the Son reciprocally love one another."[20] It's because of this eternal dynamic of self-gift that we can say that God is love.

What are the features of this Trinitarian love, the purest love in existence? The first is a free and total gift of self, with the outpouring, reception, and response that we just saw. There is also a permanent union of persons, for "the distinction between the Father, the Son, and the Holy Ghost would be unreal if it were less than Personal; their Unity would be unreal if it were less than substantial."[21] And finally, there is a fecundity, a spiritual fruitfulness: the Holy Spirit proceeds from the Father and the Son in their mutual outpouring. Compare these three elements to the three questions asked in a Catholic wedding.[22] First, the priest or deacon asks the couple, "Have you come here to enter into Marriage without coercion, freely and wholeheartedly?" That is, is your gift of self both free and total? Second, "Are you prepared, as you follow the path of Marriage, to love and honor each other for as long as you both shall live?" That is, is this union of persons to be permanent? And finally, "Are you prepared to accept children lovingly from God and to bring them up according to the law of Christ and his Church?" That is, is this love to be fruitful?

Even among animals, there's something selfless about sex. That's a strange claim, given all of the selfishness that we see both in the animal kingdom and the human realm. What I mean is what the philosopher Leon Kass has pointed out: that "whereas eating serves the good of the being that eats, sexuality — however pleasurable to the animal participants — serves mainly the good of those beings that issue from this sexual union (and, indirectly, the 'good of the species')."[23] In some instances, such as the salmon's swimming upstream to "spawn and die," the adult animals give themselves entirely for the sake of the young.[24] The design for human sexuality includes and is above this, more noble and more dignified than what we find in the animal kingdom. But we're capable of dragging sexuality down beneath the level of animals, of corrupting sex into something ultimately selfish. This isn't faithful to the other person, or to our own nature (including both our biological wiring and our spiritual destiny), or even to the act of sexual intercourse. And so the various nos of marriage protect us from hurting ourselves, each other, and sex.

Truly selfless human sexuality is one of the most vivid images of the Trinity available to us. Just as we understand the meaning of the term "God the Father" through our experiences of human fatherhood (see Eph 3:14–15), healthy Christian sexuality should help us to understand God better, by making concepts such as "total self-gift" and "fruitful love" a great deal more concrete and believable. God the Creator has created us with the capacity to become procreators. This is the yes so often missing from our discussions of sexuality. It's not about how much you can get away with; it's about how well you can make the Trinity visible through your love for your spouse and for your family. Alongside your spouse, you can complete the image of God in a way that's impossible for you, with your half of a reproductive system, to do on your own.

The Coin of God

A small international controversy was sparked in 2001 when a

Scottish national was arrested in Thailand for urinating on a picture of King Rama IX. The man was deported after serving time in prison, but his punishment could have been much worse: It is a capital crime in Thailand to deface images of the royals, including on currency.[25] Why does the country take such crimes so seriously? Because desecrating an image of the king is considered an attack on the king himself. The incident recalls a scene from the Gospels. When the scribes and the Pharisees hoped to create an international incident of their own between Rome and the preacher from Galilee, they did so by asking Jesus, "Is it lawful for us to give tribute to Caesar, or not?" Recognizing the trap, Jesus responded, "Show me a coin. Whose likeness and inscription has it?" When they rightly answered "Caesar's," he said to them, "Then render to Caesar the things that are Caesar's, and to God the things that are God's" (Lk 20:22–25).

On the surface, Christ appears merely to be pointing out that the Pharisees were carrying Roman money, a painful reminder for the Jewish people, who were forbidden to mint their own coins.[26] But Jesus is saying something more. The coins were made by Caesar and for Caesar, in order that he might collect taxes. And one of the ways we know this is from the "likeness and inscription" on it. We know that the coins are by and for him because Caesar's image is on them. Read in that light, when Jesus says to render "to God the things that are God's," his listeners should be asking, "Where do we find God's image and likeness?" The answer, of course, is within ourselves. And so, just as we give those Roman coins to Caesar, we ought to give our whole selves to God.

"*Veni Creator Spiritus*," a hymn dating back to the ninth century, captures this beautifully in its opening line: "Come, Creator Spirit, visit the souls of thy people, fill with grace from on high the hearts which thou hast created."[27] Our hearts are made by and for God. This is both the deepest aspect of our destiny and a reminder of the dignity of our neighbor. Saint John says that if anyone "says, 'I love God,' and hates his brother, he is a liar; for he who does not love his brother whom he has seen, cannot love God whom he has not seen" (1 Jn 4:20). Strong words, but warranted. You are a "coin of God," minted for eternal glory. So is your neighbor also created in the divine likeness and prepared, as we will see in chapter 8, for divine glory. You cannot desecrate the image of God in your neighbor without assaulting God, any more than you can deface Thai currency without dishonoring the Thai king.

CHAPTER 6
You, a Child of God

In the Prologue to his Gospel, John says that Jesus was rejected by "his own people," but that "to all who received him, who believed in his name, he gave power to become children of God; who were born, not of blood nor of the will of the flesh nor of the will of man, but of God" (1:11–13). A few chapters later, Jesus explains to Nicodemus that "unless one is born of water and the Spirit, he cannot enter the kingdom of God" (3:5). This language of birth is the language of becoming a child. You were born once as a child of your parents, and as a child of this world. You are born again in baptism as a child of God. Baptism is the washing of water and the Spirit. Saint Paul, in describing the cloud of the Holy Spirit leading the Israelites through the parted Red Sea, speaks of it as the moment in which "all passed through the sea, and all were baptized into Moses in the cloud and in the sea" (1 Cor 10:2–3). And John ends the conversation with Nicodemus by saying, "After this Jesus and his disciples went into the land of Judea; there he remained with them and baptized" (Jn 3:22).

Not everyone understands this connection between baptism and being a child of God. In 1989, the best-selling author and Reformed Baptist pastor John Piper gave a thirty-three-minute sermon titled "How to Become a Child of God," and at no point did he so much as mention baptism.[1] So why should we look to baptism instead of some other point in the spiritual life? There are at least four reasons. First, because it is in baptism that the Holy Spirit is imparted to us. This is exactly the difference between Jesus' baptism and the baptism of John, as Saint Paul explains to the Corinthians in Acts 19:1–7. When the crowd at Pentecost asked Peter and the rest of the apostles, "Brethren, what shall we do?" Peter replied to them, "Repent, and be baptized every one of you in the name of Jesus Christ for the forgiveness of your sins; and you shall receive the gift of the Holy Spirit" (Acts 2:37–38). Peter's response also points to a second reason: that in baptism we find the forgiveness of our sins. The forgiveness of our sins was accomplished by Christ's death on the cross, but the merits of his atonement must be applied to us (which is why both Protestants and Catholics speak of people "getting saved," and not simply being saved from before their birth). That's why Ananias tells Saint Paul, after his conversion, "Rise and be baptized, and wash away your sins, calling on his name" (Acts 22:16). Saint Paul connects both justification and sanctification to baptism in 1 Corinthians 6:11, when he says, "You were washed, you were sanctified, you were justified in the name of the Lord Jesus Christ and in the Spirit of our God." And Saint Peter puts it the most bluntly. After speaking of Noah's ark, he says, "Baptism, which corresponds to this, now saves you" (1 Pt 3:21).

Finally, baptism is our doorway to the Church. In response to Peter's sermon on Pentecost, "those who received his word were baptized, and there were added that day about three thousand souls" (Acts 2:41). Added to what? The Church. Added how? Through baptism. Another way of saying this is that, in baptism, we put on Christ and become a part of the Body of Christ. Saint Paul writes that "in Christ Jesus you are all sons of God, through faith. For as many of you as were baptized into Christ have put on Christ" (Gal 3:26–27). Elsewhere, Paul compares baptism to circumcision (the rite that made a male a full member of Israel), saying, "In him also you were circumcised with a circumcision made without hands, by putting off the body of flesh in the circumcision of Christ; and you were buried with him in baptism, in which you were also raised with him through faith in the working of God, who raised him from the dead" (Col 2:11–12). Each of these four aspects fulfills God's promise through the prophet Ezekiel:

> For I will take you from the nations, and gather you from all the countries, and bring you into your own land. I will sprinkle clean water upon you, and you shall be clean from all your uncleannesses, and from all your idols I will cleanse you. A new heart I will give you, and a new spirit I will put within you; and I will take out of your flesh the heart of stone and give you a heart of flesh. And I will put my spirit within you, and cause you to walk in my statutes and be careful to observe my ordinances. You shall dwell in the land which I gave to your fathers; and you shall be my people, and I will be your God. (Ezekial 36:24–28)

Through this sprinkling of clean water, we have been cleansed from our wickedness, strengthened for the journey, and made the People of God.

It's not a coincidence that at Jesus' baptism we first hear the words "You are my beloved Son; with you I am well pleased" (Lk 3:22). Jesus has no need for repentance (see Mt 3:14), and he is the beloved Son of the Father before his baptism (Lk 1:35). And so, Jesus is coming to the waters of Jordan to be baptized, not because he needs John's "baptism of repentance" (Mk 1:4), but because he wants to sanctify the baptismal waters, raising Christian baptism to a level beyond what John could offer (Acts 19:1–7).[2] In other words, it is not Jesus who needs to hear from the Father that he is God's beloved son. His identity is secure within the love of the Father. Rather, it is we who need to be reminded of this — both about Jesus and about our roles as beloved sons and daughters of God. So how do we allow that identity as children of God to permeate our lives more thoroughly?

Living as a Child of God

The most direct explanation of what it means to be a child of God comes from the so-called parable of the prodigal son. It's one of the most famous of Jesus' parables, but it's also one of the most badly misnamed. That title (which appears nowhere in Scripture) suggests that the most important character in the story is the younger son, the prodigal. Moreover, it suggests that the most important characteristic about him is his wastefulness: The term *prodigal* derives from a Latin word meaning "wasteful" or "lavish."[3] But to understand the true meaning of the text, and the oddity of its seemingly abrupt ending, we must recognize the context. Tax collectors and sinners were drawing near to hear Jesus, and the scribes and Pharisees were appalled, murmuring, "This man receives sinners and eats with them" (Lk 15:1-2). Jesus responds by telling the Pharisees three parables, the last of which is the so-called parable of the prodigal son.

That's our first clue that this isn't about the younger brother: The audience is the scribes and Pharisees, who are represented in the parable by the older brother, not the younger. The content of the other two parables (those of the lost coin and the lost sheep) also signals this. These are each about something beloved, a coin or a sheep (representing sinners), that goes missing and is carefully recovered by its owner (representing God). But each parable ends with the owner calling his or her friends and neighbors to "rejoice with me, for I have found my sheep [or the coin] which was lost" (Lk 15:6, 9). And the lesson of each parable ends with an explanation of the joy in heaven over returning sinners: "Just so, I tell you, there is joy before the angels of God over one sinner who repents" (Lk 15:10). In other words, these stories only seem to be about the coin and the sheep. They're really about how we react when a person goes spiritually astray and how we react when he returns.

Jesus is showing the Pharisees something about the Father, and by extension, showing something deeply awry in their own spirits. They're scoffing when they should be rejoicing. When

Jesus asks, "What man of you, having a hundred sheep, if he has lost one of them, does not leave the ninety-nine in the wilderness, and go after the one which is lost, until he finds it?" (Lk 15:4), the answer is: none of us. To us, that sort of behavior seems reckless and wasteful. Why risk losing an entire flock by chasing after one stray? In other words, the true "prodigal" in each of the three stories is the Father, who chases after his lost sheep and who lavishly pours out his mercy on his children even after they stray.

Indeed, this is how Jesus introduces the parable: "There was a man who had two sons" (Lk 15:11). This parable is about both sons, but it is even more about that man, who represents God the Father. And the two sons are much more similar than they might appear on the surface. The story begins with the younger son saying to his father, "Father, give me the share of property that falls to me." He is, in essence, demanding his inheritance, treating his father as dead to him. It's a shocking and scandalous request, yet the father "divided his living between them" (Lk 15:12). But notice that shift: Instead of just giving the younger son his half, the father doles out the inheritance to both sons.

Both sons, the self-righteous one and the obviously sinful one, have treated their father as if he's dead to them. And the similarities don't end there. The younger son goes far from the father, off into a "far country," where he "squander[s] his property in loose living" (Lk 15:13). After a famine strikes the land, he's reduced to taking care of swine and eating the pigs' food to avoid starvation. That sounds miserable to us, but the level of sheer scandal in Jesus' description is lost on our non-kosher ears. Jews couldn't even touch pigs, and here is a Jew so low that he's away from his homeland, herding swine and even sharing food with them. Those are details that Jesus' original audience of Pharisees and scribes of the Mosaic law would not have missed.

Having hit rock bottom, the younger son sees the folly of his sinful ways, remembers his father's mercy, and resolves to return to him to say, "Father, I have sinned against heaven and before you; I am no longer worthy to be called your son; treat me as one of your hired servants" (Lk 15:18–19). His sinfulness has damaged his sense of sonship, as he knows he's unworthy to be a son of the father. Yet he can't help himself, and he addresses the father as "Father" anyway. On some level, even as he is in the literal mire, he's cognizant that his father's forgiveness is greater than even the greatest of our sins. That's a deeply rooted sense of sonship.

And so he attempts his plan, but "while he was yet at a distance, his father saw him and had compassion, and ran and embraced him and kissed him" (Lk 15:20). The impression of these words is that the father has been eagerly watching and waiting for his son. And when the son speaks his rehearsed lines about his unworthiness even to be a son, the father will have none of it, saying to the servants: "Bring quickly the best robe, and put it on him; and put a ring on his hand, and shoes on his feet; and bring the fatted calf and kill it, and let us eat and make merry; for this my son was dead, and is alive again; he was lost, and is found" (Lk 15:22–24).

The father rejoices in the return of his son, and it's only at this point that the prior two parables make sense. Throwing a party over the recovery of a lost sheep or a lost coin might seem excessive, but it's more than appropriate for a son risen from the dead. Jesus' use of resurrection language is also significant: We can cut ourselves off from the Father and become spiritually dead. Saint Paul reminds us that we have each experienced the kind of resurrection the father and son are celebrating here, for "you he made alive, when you were dead through the trespasses and sins in which you once walked, following the course of this world, following the prince of the power of the air, the spirit that is now at work in the sons of disobedience" (Eph 2:1–2). To live as a son of God is both to share in Jesus' resurrection and to be resurrected ourselves from the death of sin to the life of grace.

There's a notable absence from the celebration, however. The elder brother misses the party, because he is "in the field" (Lk

15:25). The location is significant. He's not in the house, as a son. He's in the field, as a slave. And in this way, he closely resembles his younger brother, who, before his reversion, "went and joined himself to one of the citizens of that country, who sent him into his fields to feed swine" (Lk 15:15). The elder brother has received his inheritance and has also gone out to work the fields like a slave. While he may not have gone as far from the house as his younger brother did, in a sense he's much further away. After learning of the celebration over his brother's return, his reaction is not one of joy, but of anger, and he refuses to enter the house. His father responds by once again going out of the house after his straying son, entreating him to come in (Lk 15:26–28).

The elder son's response is worth listening to carefully: "Behold, these many years I have served you, and I never disobeyed your command; yet you never gave me a kid, that I might make merry with my friends. But when this son of yours came, who has devoured your living with harlots, you killed for him the fatted calf!" (Lk 15:29–30). Whereas the younger brother begins by calling out "Father," the elder says only "Behold." His entire objection is that of a slave: he hasn't received a big enough bonus for his hard work and his careful obedience to orders. And he cannot even refer to his returning brother as his brother, but instead calls him "this son of yours." Not a word in his entire objection hints at his being either his father's son or the elder brother of the returned son.

The father gently corrects his son on three points: "Son, you are always with me, and all that is mine is yours. It was fitting to make merry and be glad, for this your brother was dead, and is alive; he was lost, and is found" (Lk 15:31–32). It's a reminder of the elder's sonship: He has become so caught up in legalistically obeying his father that he has lost a sense of being a son. It's also a reminder that to be a son of the father is to a be brother to every other child of the father. Too often, we treat theological questions about the love of God as radically distinct from the love of neighbor. Yet the clear message of Jesus' parable is precisely that to be a son of the Father is to be a brother of your neighbor.

This is a recurring theme in Jesus' preaching. For example, when he is asked what the "great commandment in the law" is, he replies, "You shall love the Lord your God with all your heart, and with all your soul, and with all your mind. This is the great and first commandment. And a second is like it, You shall love your neighbor as yourself. On these two commandments depend all the law and the prophets" (Mt 22:37–40). What does Jesus mean that the second great commandment "is like" the first? He means that the second flows from the first: Love of neighbor is the appropriate response to the love of God, so anyone living the first great commandment can see the need to live the second, and anyone living both well will be doing what the entire Mosaic law was trying to encourage. Saint John makes the point this way: "In this is love, not that we loved God but that he loved us and sent his Son to be the expiation for our sins. Beloved, if God so loved us, we also ought to love one another" (1 Jn 4:10–11). So, our experience of being a beloved son should give rise to being a loving brother to those in need. Saint John goes as far as to say that anyone who says, "I love God" but hates his brother "is a liar; for he who does not love his brother whom he has seen, cannot love God whom he has not seen. And this commandment we have from him, that he who loves God should love his brother also" (1 Jn 4:20–21).

The Humility of a Child of God

In chapter 2, we saw that Jesus' identity as the Son of God was a proclamation of both his great power (equality with God the Father) and his great humility (a total reliance on the Father). We, too, are promised a divine inheritance. But we, too, need to follow the example of Jesus Christ in his humility, as Saint Paul tells the Philippians:

> Let each of you look not only to his own interests, but also to the interests of others. Have this mind among

yourselves, which was in Christ Jesus, who, though he
was in the form of God, did not count equality with
God a thing to be grasped, but emptied himself, taking
the form of a servant, being born in the likeness of men.
And being found in human form he humbled himself
and became obedient unto death, even death on a cross.
(2:4–8)

This posture of humility is a challenge to our modern way of
thinking.[4] We imagine that God calls the holiest, most qualified individuals to positions of authority. Isn't this one of the
major reasons that male headship in the family is so controversial, since it seems to suggest that the wife is inferior in some
respect to her husband? And don't we often find ourselves fall-
ing into the trap of thinking either that the ordained are holier
than we laypeople are or that true holiness is only for those who
are priests or pastors, sisters or monks, or in some other way in
"full-time ministry"?

And yet, throughout salvation history, we find God raising
up those who, by any external standard, seem instead to be particularly unqualified. The clearest example of this is in Judges 7,
after Gideon has raised an army of some 32,000 men to fight the
Midianites. God stops him and prevents him from proceeding
into battle — not because Gideon's army is too small, but because it is too large. God says to Gideon, "The people with you
are too many for me to give the Midianites into their hand, lest
Israel vaunt themselves against me, saying, 'My own hand has
delivered me'" (Jgs 7:2). In other words, it would be far too easy
to omit God's providence from the picture and for the men to
glory in their own natural gifts and talents. And so God first has
Gideon dismiss whoever is afraid and wants to go home. Then
he culls the army in a much stranger way. He has Gideon take
the men down to the river to drink water, and he is instructed to
keep anyone who "laps the water with his tongue, as a dog laps"
(Jgs 7:5) and let everyone else go. The army of 32,000 men is

quickly reduced in this way to an army of 300 weirdos who never learned the proper way to drink water.[5] When Gideon and his band of weirdos achieve a major military victory over the Midianites, there can be no question that God is the one in control.

Consider the many times throughout the Old Testament, the New Testament, and today, in which the holiest people weren't the most powerful ones, and the most powerful people weren't the holiest. Not everyone who has great faith is called to an official position in the Church, and not everyone with a position in the Church is faithful. The apostles flee when Christ is arrested, one of them denies him three times, and one of them betrays him for money. Yet Christ's female followers stay close to him until the end and beyond. This isn't a mistake: It's not as if, with the benefit of hindsight, Christ should have chosen the women for his apostles instead. Remember Jesus' words to the apostles: "Did I not choose you, the twelve, and one of you is a devil?" (Jn 6:70). It may well be that the women were aided by not having an official status — that the temptation of power would have corrupted them, as it did (and continues to do) to so many of Jesus' male followers. But such humility is hard to accept. Even when we talk about the importance of laypeople taking ownership over their faith, our first reaction is often to find some official ministry or office to occupy. But the Virgin Mary and Christ's most faithful followers embody a different model.

In the Holy Family, Joseph is the head, yet he is undoubtedly the least qualified to be in charge. His wife is the Virgin Mary, prophesied in Scripture, the Ark of the New Covenant. His son is God himself. Yet, when God wishes to communicate messages to the family, he does so not by having the baby Jesus break into speech, or having the angel Gabriel go back to Mary (as he had done before Joseph took Mary into his home), but by sending an angel to Joseph in a dream. This happens three times. First, the angel tells Joseph that his family must flee to Egypt in the middle of the night (see Mt 2:13). Next, the angel tells him that it's time for his family to return to Israel (Mt 2:20). Finally, the angel tells Joseph to settle his family in Nazareth rather than in Bethlehem (Mt 2:22).

Imagine the experience of that first dream for Mary, being awakened by her husband in the middle of the night and told that they had to leave *immediately* to go to a foreign country. At the time, there was no clarity about when they would be able to return, or how God would communicate this — only the ominous warning that Herod wanted to murder their baby. Trusting an angel directly from God is one thing. Trusting the dreams of your newly awakened husband is quite another. It would be easy to doubt Joseph, to suspect that his dream was the result of an overactive imagination, or the normal anxieties of new fatherhood, or perhaps even a bit of jealousy at not being the recipient of any annunciations. But instead, Mary responds with immediate trust, and Joseph "rose and took the child and his mother by night, and departed to Egypt" (Mt 2:14).

In Mary, we find the perfect example of the behavior of a child of God. Her radical trust and obedience come from her faith, her belief that God "has scattered the proud in the imagination of their hearts, he has put down the mighty from their thrones, and exalted those of low degree; he has filled the hungry with good things, and the rich he has sent empty away" (Lk 1:51–53). Mary's is a belief in the God of David rather than the false gods of Goliath. She shows us what it is to be a son or daughter of God and reveals the kind of trust we are each called to have.

Success and Failure

Understanding yourself as a son or daughter of God also revolutionizes your gauge for success or failure. If your identity is overly rooted in your job, if that's how you define who you are, you'll find it hard to retire. If things turn south at work, if the projects you're working on don't go as well as you'd like, that becomes a devastating tragedy. It's not just that you've failed at work or that the business that you're working for is failing. You, as you've defined yourself, are a failure.

Nor are only those who work outside the home prone to this temptation. Not a few parents have invested so much of their identity in raising their children that the sins and mistakes of their kids, even the failings common to particular stages of their growth, become unacceptable. Often, this is less about the good of the kid (who may well benefit from the experience of seeking forgiveness after sinning, or learning from failing, and so forth) and more about the way that the child's failings reflect upon the parent. If "who you are" is the mother or father of this child, then that child's successes and failures become your successes and failures to an unhealthy degree.

The rise of social media has exacerbated this problem, as we (particularly younger generations) increasingly look online to find our identity and our worth. Bruce Feiler noted in a 2014 *New York Times* editorial, "We are deep enough into the so-cial-media era to begin to recognize certain patterns among its users. Foremost among them is a mass anxiety of approval seek-ing and popularity tracking that seems far more suited to a high school prom than a high-functioning society."[6] This is a genu-inely alarming trend. Social scientists and psychologists have noticed "a rapid rise in rates of anxiety and depression" among young people today, compared with earlier generations.[7] The numbers paint a shocking picture: "[Teenage] boys' depression increased by 21% between 2012 and 2015, and girls' increased by 50%."[8] This astonishing surge of mental illness is linked directly to social media usage. Studies have found that heavy social me-dia usage is "significantly associated with increased depression"[9] and that reducing your time on social media outlets to ten min-utes per platform per day "leads to significant decreases in both depression and loneliness."[10] In fact, "subjects who started out with moderately severe depressive symptoms saw declines down to the mild range by the simple expedient of limiting social me-dia use for three weeks." One study participant later explained, "Not comparing my life to the lives of others had a much stron-ger impact than I expected, and I felt a lot more positive about myself during those weeks."[11]

Looking to the world for that ultimate validation is a losing gambit. In contrast, if your identity is rooted in Christ, and in being a child of God alongside Christ, the question of success and failure takes on a completely different light. Jesus promises us that "in me you may have peace. In the world you have tribulation; but be of good cheer, I have overcome the world" (Jn 16:33). He already achieved success on the cross and in his rising from the tomb. He defeated sin and death, the two most fearsome foes of humanity. And he offers us the opportunity to join his team — a team that's not just winning but has (in a very real sense) already won. As Saint John says, "Whatever is born of God overcomes the world; and this is the victory that overcomes the world, our faith. Who is it that overcomes the world but he who believes that Jesus is the Son of God?" (1 Jn 5:4–5). This perspective changes everything. It's the difference between "I'm a failure, because my work performance is lagging," and "My work performance is lagging, but that's a small cross on my road to eternal life." The number of likes and tweets you get simply won't matter as much, and you'll feel less obliged to keep up with the Joneses or to "outparent" the parents next door. You'll be able to breathe a little easier, for finding your identity in Christ is liberating. The victory has already been won.

Praying Like a Child of God

Let's go back to the parable of the prodigal son. Between his verbal restoration of the elder son's relationship with his father and his younger brother, the father shows the absurdity of his elder son's frustration, with the reminder that "all that I have is yours." If you are a part of the family, then the family business and the family house and everything that belongs to the family belong to you. You don't work the land because you're getting a set wage and maybe, if you try hard enough, a goat. You work the land because it's your land, and you want it to flourish.

When we look at how we pray, do we pray as slaves or as

children of the Father? When you approach the God of heaven, do you do so with an awareness that all that is his is yours? When the apostles approach Jesus and say, "Lord, teach us to pray, as John taught his disciples" (Lk 11:1), Jesus responds by telling them to call on God as Father, giving them the prayer we now know as the Lord's Prayer or the Our Father (see Lk 11:2–4; Mt 6:9–13). That is, Jesus wants our posture of prayer to be of children approaching the Father. And that's an incredibly powerful posture, as he goes on to illustrate: "What father among you, if his son asks for a fish, will instead of a fish give him a serpent; or if he asks for an egg, will give him a scorpion? If you then, who are evil, know how to give good gifts to your children, how much more will the heavenly Father give the Holy Spirit to those who ask him!" (Lk 11:11–13). That last line is worth considering very carefully, because we often overlook the Trinitarian implications of the divine promise.

When the Father says, "All that I have is yours," he doesn't mean just stuff. His promise means that the Father, the Son, and the Holy Spirit are ours for the asking, and so our begging for the Spirit is exactly the sort of tapping into this spiritual treasury that the Father envisions and encourages. And just as the Father sends the Spirit, the Spirit leads us into a deeper intimacy with the Father, and a deeper awareness of our sonship. In the words of Saint Paul, "You did not receive the spirit of slavery to fall back into fear, but you have received the spirit of sonship. When we cry, 'Abba! Father!' it is the Spirit himself bearing witness with our spirit that we are children of God" (Rom 8:15–16).[12]

Our relationship to God is not that of servants or slaves, desperately trying to win the approval of the Master. Rather, we are children already loved by the Father, already promised every good gift, up to and including the glories of heaven, and for whom even the greatest sufferings are trials permitted in love by God as a means of strengthening us and making us more the creatures we were meant to be. As children, we are not simply entries on some divine spreadsheet, or anonymous numbers in some master plan. We are each individually and uniquely loved. We have a God who calls us each by name.

CHAPTER 7
You, and Your New Name

At the time I write this, my daughter is late — five days past her due date, to be precise. As a result, my wife and I have had plenty of time to think about what we're going to name her. There's a joke that says, "You never know how many people you dislike until you have to name your child," but it's perhaps more accurate to say simply that you don't realize how strong your associations are with certain names until you consider giving one of those names to your child. In our case, we knew from the start that we wanted a beautiful Catholic name, preferably one to honor a saint. We also wanted to avoid anything that was too trendy or popular, or that would be easily mocked or had negative associations. The three left standing after months of deliberation are Stella Maris (an ancient Marian title), Gemma (in honor of Saint Gemma Galgani, an Italian mystic), or Karolina (for Karol Wojtyła, better known as Saint John Paul II).

This was the most seriously that we've personally had to grapple with the complex reality of naming, but we are hardly alone. As the *New York Times* reported back in 2013, "Baby naming has become an industry — with paid consultants, books, Web sites brimming with trend data, and academic studies exploring correlations between baby names and future success."[1] As an industry, baby naming has exploded over the last few decades. And although these excesses can be rightly critiqued, we should recognize what they get right: that "the selection of a child's name, which he or she will likely bear for the rest of his or her life, is one of the most significant decisions parents will ever make."[2]

One of the reasons we're still undecided about our daughter's name is that we want to get to meet her first and see which name seems to "fit." Naming is profoundly personal, which is why it's troubling that you can now pay someone else to name your baby for you, just to avoid the anxiety.[3] As humans, we have strong associations with words and even sounds. In the "Boy named Sue" phenomenon, boys with traditionally feminine names were found to be more prone to disruptive behavior.[4] But this is only the tip of the iceberg: "Individuals systematically map the linguistic properties of words onto the physical characteristics of shapes" in a way that transcends language and culture.[5] People whose names seem to "match" their faces (e.g. a man with angular features named Kirk, or a man with rounder features named Bob) are viewed as more trustworthy than "mismatched" names, so much so that one study found that "Senatorial candidates earn 10% more votes when their names fit their faces very well."[6] So naming is important, but it's also personal: There's no one-size-fits-all formula.

In chapter 3, we looked at the rich significance and meaning of particular divine names: the unspeakable name YHWH, the "name" Emmanuel, and Jesus, the name "by which we must be saved" (Acts 4:10–12). But what can we say about our own names? There are four major points worth noting. First, in naming, we recognize the distinctiveness of a thing. Second, and related to the first, it's for this reason that we care when others forget (or never bother to learn) our names. We want to be known, and a crucial aspect of being known is tied to our names. Third, name changes signify changes at the most foundational level of identity, and this is why Scripture takes them so seriously. And finally, the scriptural promise of a new name given to us by God is thus ultimately an affirmation (a) that God knows us in a radical and utterly unique, distinct way; and (b) that our fullest, truest identity can be found only in him and revealed by him. To flesh out these four points, it helps to go all the way back to the beginning.

Adam

On the very first page of the Bible, creation begins when "God said, 'Let there be light'; and there was light" (Gn 1:3). God creates through speech. In the next chapter, God creates Adam and tasks him with the tending of the Garden of Eden. He then gives him a curious task, the naming of things:

> Then the LORD God said, "It is not good that the man should be alone; I will make him a helper fit for him." So out of the ground the LORD God formed every beast of the field and every bird of the air, and brought them to the man to see what he would call them; and whatever the man called every living creature, that was its name. The man gave names to all cattle, and to the birds of the air, and to every beast of the field; but for the man there was not found a helper fit for him. (Genesis 2:18–20)

As he names each creature, Adam's relationship with the animal changes. We continue to experience this in our relationships with animals. Margo DeMello, a professor of "anthrozoology" (the study of man's interactions with animals), writes that "in the West, at least, one cannot be a pet and not have a name. Naming an animal incorporates him or her into the human social world and allows us to use their name as a term of address and a term of reference."[7] Naming is one of the crucial differences between the animals that we keep as pets and the animals that we eat or perform scientific research on. Conversely, the refusal to give livestock or research animals individual names isn't an oversight; it's a tacit recognition that "we do not eat those with whom we have a personal relationship."[8] Marc Bekoff, one of Jane Goodall's long-time collaborators, points out that naming animals "immediately creates an identity and a connection; a name indicates that we are meeting an individual being with feelings and an autobiography. A name can open neurological floodgates of emotion."[9]

Naming also creates a sense of order and what the Bible refers to as "dominion." As Senator Ben Sasse pointed out, contrary to the common misconception, the Frankenstein monster is not named Frankenstein, because "Shelley never gave the monster a name. This was a purposeful omission, which has now become a convention in horror movies. A powerful entity with no name is unnerving." Naming something, in contrast, "gives us a handle on it. Adam brought the Garden of Eden under his dominion by the act of naming the animals."[10]

Through naming, man's relationship to animals is revealed, as is his distinction from them. The instruction to name the animals is the second thing God commanded of man. The first is to "be fruitful and multiply, and fill the earth and subdue it; and have dominion over the fish of the sea and over the birds of the air and over every living thing that moves upon the earth" (Gn 1:28). These two sets of instructions, to name things and to have dominion over them, end up being closely related. As Pope Saint John Paul II explained, these two chapters depict "man's original solitude." By naming things, Adam is simultaneously discovering the world around him and, by extension, learning something of himself and his dissimilarity from the rest of visible creation: "Self-knowledge develops at the same rate as knowledge of the world, of all the visible creatures, of all the living beings to which man has given a name to affirm his own dissimilarity with regard to them. In this way, consciousness reveals man as the one who possesses a cognitive faculty as regards the visible world."[11]

Albert Einstein remarked that "of what is significant in one's own existence one is hardly aware," for "what does a fish know about the water in which he swims all his life?"[12] Only by peering out of the "water" of his own limited existence can man come to notice the waters surrounding him. John Paul II's point is similar. In coming to understand the world and its inhabitants, Adam can see himself as distinct and dissimilar. In naming a particular bird or animal, he recognizes its uniqueness and the way it is distinct from other types of animals. In this way he comes to understand himself. As G. K. Chesterton observed, "It is exactly when we do regard man as an animal that we know he is not an animal. It is precisely when we do try to picture him as a sort of horse on its hind legs, that we suddenly realise that he must be something as miraculous as the winged horse that towered up into the clouds of heaven."[13]

In naming the animals, Adam can see how he is unlike each animal, but also how he is unlike all other animals. The most crucial difference is the one we are perhaps most likely to gloss over: Adam is the kind of creature who names the animals; none of the animals possesses such a cognitive capacity. The philosopher Leon Kass makes a similar observation: that, of all the species surrounding us, "none of these knows anything about animal rights or curbs its appetite out of compassion or respect for fellow creatures."[14] It is precisely those moments in which we show the most attention to, and respect for, the animal kingdom that we properly recognize ourselves as radically unlike the animals for which we care.

All this to say that the act of naming simultaneously helps us to understand who or what we're naming *and* to understand ourselves better. A similar point can be made about the relationship between the sexes: Much of what we understand of what it is to be a man or a woman comes precisely from our understanding of the opposite sex. And that, indeed, is the very next lesson Adam will learn. Even after naming all the animals, "there was not found a helper fit for him," and so God takes a rib from the sleeping Adam to create a woman (Gn 2:21–23). Here again we see the themes of unity and distinction. The man delights in the woman both because of how she's like him ("bone of my bones and flesh of my flesh") and because of how she's different. In naming Eve, he sees a person like himself, not a subhuman creature like the animals he had encountered thus far. As Matthew Henry (1662–1714) famously explained, "The woman was made of a rib out of the side of Adam; not made out of his head to top him, nor out of his feet to be trampled upon by him, but out of his side to be equal with him, under his arm to be protected, and near his heart to be beloved."[15]

Each stage of the progression in Genesis so far — from the creation of the universe, to man's discovery of the natural world and his place in it, to the discovery of sexual distinction and the relationship between man and woman — is described as coming about through language and, in the latter two cases, specifically through naming. The message is that there's something particularly powerful about naming, even compared with other aspects of language. Whether we're naming a species or a human being, naming is "directly a form of knowing," since it "selects, discriminates, identifies, locates, orders, arranges, systematizes."[16] If you refer to border collies and hounds as "dogs," but don't refer to wolves or cats as dogs, you're making a statement about collies and hounds, but you're also making a statement about wolves and cats. Some property or set of properties distinguishes these animals from one another. Likewise, when you take the trouble to learn someone's name, you signal that you recognize that person as distinct from the mass of humanity.

This is close to the foundation of human knowing. One of the first tasks a child undertakes in organizing the world of sense experience is to learn the names of things. All science is built upon this, for without it, you cannot distinguish between various genera or solar systems. But naming isn't simply about taking the world in, or sorting our sensory experiences; it's about entering into the world in a new way. Ludwig Wittgenstein (1889–1951) has pointed out that languages, like rules, are never purely "private." There's a difference between thinking you're obeying a rule and actually obeying it, or thinking you're using a word correctly and actually using it correctly.[17] To suggest otherwise — to say that words mean whatever we want them to mean at a particular moment — is to reject the intelligibility of language. That's the position of Humpty Dumpty in Lewis Carroll's *Through the Looking-Glass.* Alice's confusion over his use of the word *glory* (which he misuses to mean "a nice knock-down argument") leads to this exchange:

> "When I use a word," Humpty Dumpty said, in rather a scornful tone, "it means just what I choose it to mean — neither more nor less."
>
> "The question is," said Alice, "whether you can make words mean so many different things."
>
> "The question is," said Humpty Dumpty, "which is to be master — that's all."[18]

Such an arrogant approach to language quickly descends into nonsense. The truth is, none of us are wholly masters of language. We can invent or redefine a term, but we can do so coherently only if we can define it in the existing language. Humpty Dumpty is able to say "*'Twas brillig, and the slithy toves / did gyre and gimble in the wabe,*" but only by painstakingly translating all of the nonsense terms.[19]

The world of Humpty Dumpty is in stark contrast to the world of Adam. The story of Genesis is the story of the very foundations of our experience of reality. Names are more than an organizational tool: they both express and create a relationship between the one who names and the one who is named. We've seen this with Adam and the animals, and then more profoundly with Adam and his wife. But there's one more dimension of naming, this time in Genesis 3–4: the birth of a child. "Now Adam knew Eve his wife, and she conceived and bore Cain [*Qayin,* קַיִן], saying, 'I have gotten [*qanah,* קָנָה] a man with the help of the LORD'" (Gn 4:1). The birth and naming of Cain creates a new status between parents and child, and therefore between the parents and each other. It's for this reason that Adam went from calling his wife Woman to calling her Eve [*Chavvah*, חַוָּה], a name believed to mean "Life," "because she was the mother of all living" (Gn 3:20). Even though we know the first couple as Adam and Eve, the first name Adam gave his wife was Woman, expressing something of his relationship with her; the second name reflects this new relationship.

Each of these three sets of dynamics — parent and child, husband and wife, owner and animal — is distinct, and where these distinctions are lost or blurred, the resultant relationships are unhealthy. But each of the three have certain common features: they involve recognizing the other *as other* and as worthy. To see this, just consider the alternative. What if parents were to decline to name their baby?[20] "Such a refusal would amount to an especially brutal form of psychological child abuse," argues law professor Carlton F. W. Larson, citing the 1959 United Nations Declaration of the Rights of the Child, which states that every child "shall be entitled from his birth to a name."[21]

Names are a form of recognition of each of us as distinct, as recognized, and as worthy. Names are how we conceptually organize the universe around us, and our own name is part of our self-understanding of our place in the universe. Whether you love or hate the name that you were given, whether it was chosen because of its deep meaning or simply because your parents liked the way it sounded, your name is a core part of your self-identity. So deep is this foundation within you that your brainwaves perk up when you hear your name ... even when you're asleep.[22]

Helen

Few people since Adam have had such a powerful experience of names as Helen Keller had. Blind and deaf from a young age, she lived in a world without language. In her autobiography, she talks about how her tutor, Miss Sullivan, attempted to break into that world. At one point, Miss Sullivan gave her a doll and attempted to sign the words *doll, mug,* and *water* into her hand. Impatient with her inability to distinguish between the concepts *mug* and *water*, Helen grabbed her new doll and smashed it on the ground. She later recalled, "I was keenly delighted when I felt the fragments of the broken doll at my feet. Neither sorrow nor regret followed my passionate outburst. I had not loved the doll. In the still, dark world in which I lived there was no strong sentiment of tenderness."[23] Without language, her relationship to the doll or to *anything* of the outside world was fleeting and ephemeral. Immediately after this outburst, Miss Sullivan took Helen to the well house where she ran water over her hands while signing the word for *water*. Something clicked, and Helen recalls feeling "a misty consciousness as of something forgotten — a thrill of returning thought; and somehow the mystery of language was revealed to me. I knew then that 'w-a-t-e-r' meant the wonderful cool something that was flowing over my hand. That living word awakened my soul, gave it light, hope, joy, set it free! There were barriers still, it is true, but barriers that could in time be swept away."[24]

Returning to the house after this revelation, Helen suddenly remembered the broken doll. "I felt my way to the hearth and picked up the pieces. I tried vainly to put them together. Then my eyes filled with tears; for I realized what I had done, and for the first time I felt repentance and sorrow."[25] Once she had the name for *doll*, or at least the realization that *doll* referred to a thing with a name, Helen grasped its existence in a radical way. The doll suddenly possessed a conceptual solidity and a permanence (even when broken) that it didn't have before. It's a powerful recognition of what Adam would have learned a long time ago: that naming helps us to establish a personal relationship. It's why one of the acts of love we show toward our friends is the bestowal of nicknames, and why lovers seem to have no end of pet names. And it's why, as we'll see shortly, it's of such significance that God speaks of a private name he has for each of us.

Simon
In Luke 5, Jesus is standing by the Lake of Gennesaret, better

known as the Sea of Galilee. He's teaching, and the crowds are pressing around him "to hear the word of God" (v. 1). Spotting two empty fishing boats, he goes into one of them. The owner of the boat, Simon, is working with the other fishermen to clean their nets. This is not, as many people assume, the first encounter between Jesus and Simon. By this point, Jesus and his disciples have already been to the wedding feast in Cana, and the disciples have witnessed Jesus' driving out of the money-changers (see Jn 2). Saint Luke even mentions that Jesus had previously healed Simon's mother-in-law (4:38–39). Simon knows Jesus well enough by now to refer to him as "Master" (Lk 5:5). He's a follower of Christ in at least some loose sense, and he seems to be some-one already trusted and relied on by Jesus for a place to stay and perform miracles (Lk 4:38–41), and now for a boat from which to preach. Luke never tells us exactly what Jesus preached about from that boat, because it's what happened next that captures his (and our) attention:

> And when he had ceased speaking, he said to Simon, "Put out into the deep and let down your nets for a catch." And Simon answered, "Master, we toiled all night and took nothing! But at your word I will let down the nets." And when they had done this, they enclosed a great shoal of fish; and as their nets were breaking, they beckoned to their partners in the other boat to come and help them. And they came and filled both the boats, so that they began to sink. But when Simon Peter saw it, he fell down at Jesus' knees, saying, "Depart from me, for I am a sinful man, O Lord." For he was astonished, and all that were with him, at the catch of fish which they had taken; and so also were James and John, sons of Zebedee, who were partners with Simon. (5:4–10)

The writer Frank Sheed described Simon's reaction as "fascinat-ing." Why, Sheed asked, "was his first reaction to a vast haul of fish an overpowering sense of his own sinfulness?"[26] This isn't Simon's first encounter with Jesus. It's not his first time seeing Jesus perform a miracle. It's not even the first time a member of Simon's family has been the beneficiary of one of Christ's miracles. But there's something about this time that's different. Sheed ventures a guess: "He had seen the money-changers scourged from the Temple — and was probably delighted to see it, feeling that they were getting what they deserved. Evidently it had not occurred to him that he was a sinner himself. This time, precisely because the miracle hit home to him in all the reality of its miraculousness, he suddenly saw Christ for the first time. Seeing Christ, he at last saw himself."[27]

That last sentence, "seeing Christ, he at last saw himself," is the entire thesis of this book. If you want to know who you are, a lifetime of navel-gazing won't tell you. You can discover the answer — or at least, do it well — only by getting to know your Maker. That's the story of Simon, but it is still only part of the story. Simon, seeing himself, sees the negatives. He sees his sins and failings, his limitations, all of the ways that he's unworthy to be a follower of Jesus or even to be in his presence. Jesus sees all of this, but sees so much more. And so he responds to Simon, "Do not be afraid; henceforth you will be catching men" (Lk 5:11). In that brief reply, Jesus shows his awareness and concern for Simon's fears, and gives him a personalized call. By that, I mean that Jesus doesn't simply say, "Follow me," but he invites Simon in a way that recognizes his current state in life as a fisherman. In other words, his words suggest that Simon's personal fulfillment lies in discipleship, but that it's about Simon's becoming more and not less of who he is. This encounter, then, is about Simon's "becoming Simon" in a deeper way. But soon, Christ will call Simon to become more than Simon.

Peter

In the Gospel of Matthew, we see Jesus addressing this question of identity. He has brought his disciples to the district of Caesarea Philippi, far from the areas in which they normally ministered. When Saint Matthew mentions that "Jesus came into the district of Caesarea Philippi" (16:13), the detail is meaningless to most of us, having little or no knowledge of biblical geography. But it's actually quite a surprising detail. Jesus is a Galilean, and most of his public ministry was centered in Galilee in the north, with occasional journeys to the capital, Jerusalem, in the south. But Caesarea Philippi is some 25 miles northeast of the Sea of Galilee, basically on the northern border of Judea. It's only about 40 miles from Damascus, the capital of Syria, but about 120 miles from Jerusalem.[28] In other words, Jesus and his disciples have gone well outside their normal ambit. And for what? Neither Matthew nor Mark tells us directly (see Mk 8:27–30). But both Gospels connect this journey to a single conversation: "Now when Jesus came into the district of Caesarea Philippi, he asked his disciples, 'Who do men say that the Son of man is?' And they said, 'Some say John the Baptist, others say Elijah, and others Jeremiah or one of the prophets.' He said to them, 'But who do you say that I am?'" (Mt 16:13–15).

It's as if Jesus has taken them far from home, far from the inquiring crowds, in order to have the most important conversation of their lives. The heart of Christianity, as we've seen, is not a set of rules or laws, but an encounter with a person, Jesus Christ. The crucial question for the Twelve is the same as it is for us today: "Who do *you* say that I am?" Simon answers the question for the Twelve, saying, "You are the Christ, the Son of the living God" (Mt 16:16). Jesus responds:

> Blessed are you, Simon Bar-Jona! For flesh and blood has not revealed this to you, but my Father who is in heaven. And I tell you, you are Peter, and on this rock I will build my Church, and the gates of Hades shall not prevail against it. I will give you the keys of the kingdom of heaven, and whatever you bind on earth shall be bound in heaven, and whatever you loose on earth shall

be loosed in heaven. (16:17–19)

"Bar-Jona" (son of Jonah) appears, at first blush, to be a family name. In fact, that seems not to be the case. Simon's father's name is John, not Jonah (see Jn 1:42). More likely, the declaration of Simon as "son of Jonah" is a Jewish idiom that should be read in the context of Jesus' declaration, a few verses earlier, about the "sign of Jonah" (Mt 16:4).[29] Nevertheless, the sonship language also creates an obvious, and seemingly intentional, parallel. Simon confesses Jesus as "Son of the living God"; Jesus confesses Simon as "son of Jonah." What's the significance of this parallel? Simply that the question "Who am I?" can be fully answered only by first answering "Who is Jesus?" and then letting Jesus reveal us to ourselves.

God is the one who designed us and the only one who knows his plans for our lives. As such, we cannot fully know ourselves without first knowing him. In the words of Saint John Paul II, "God has placed in the human heart a desire to know the truth — in a word, to know himself — so that, by knowing and loving God, men and women may also come to the fullness of truth about themselves."[30] Knowing Christ more fully humanizes us. But that's not all it does. Our relationship with Jesus leads to our participation in the fullness of the two natures of Christ, "a humanization alongside a deification."[31] We'll unpack the meaning of the Christian concept of *deification* or *divinization* in the next chapter, but for now, suffice it to say that it's through Christ that we come to see both who we are and who we can be with the help of his grace.

In the case of Simon, "who he is" is Simon, and "who he can be with the help of God's grace" is Peter. It's significant that this distinction is made through a name change. Precisely because names are such a fundamental part of our identity, name changes are associated with the most important life changes. After birth, the first of these is baptism. We sometimes refer to our first names as our "Christian names," but more properly, our Christian names are the ones we received at baptism.[32] This reflects an ancient Christian practice, dating back to at least the third century, of taking a saint's name in baptism.[33] Thus, the infant Wolfgang Amadeus Mozart became Joannes Chrysostomus Wolfgangus Theophilus Mozart, in honor of Saint John Chrysostom.[34] In marriage, most women change their surnames to their husbands', signifying a new and united identity as a married couple.[35] And nearly every bishop of Rome since Pope John II in 533 has taken a new name upon becoming pope.[36]

It's the last of these that's most applicable to the scene in Matthew 16. Jesus is calling Simon to a new role in the Church, and the nature of that role is revealed not only in the changing of his name, but in the new name itself. Jesus renames Simon "Peter," a name that Jesus appears to have invented, meaning "Rock."[37] Why this name? Because "on this rock I will build my Church, and the gates of Hades shall not prevail against it" (Mt 16:18).

Just as Adam changed his wife's name to Eve (Life) "because she was the mother of all living" (Gn 3:20), Jesus now changes Simon's name to reveal the nature of his new identity. Jesus is explicitly founding his Church on Simon Peter. The Reformer John Calvin considered this idea of papal succession going back to Peter to be a thing "too childish in itself to need an answer": "For if they insist on applying everything that was said to Peter to the successors of Peter, it will follow, that they are all Satans, because our Lord once said to Peter, 'Get thee behind me, Satan, thou art an offence unto me.' It is as easy for us to retort the latter saying as for them to adduce the former."[38] What Calvin misses in his objection is that this is the whole point. Simon is radically unworthy to be called Peter; he's radically unworthy to be the rock on which Christ will build his Church. And, of course, Jesus knows this, and he even seems to wink at this fact. Just as Calvin said, Jesus refers to Peter as an "offence" or a "hindrance" (Mt 16:23). But what he fails to mention is that this occurs almost immediately after Jesus renames Simon "Peter," and the term he used is *skandalon* (σκάνδαλον), which is literally a "rock of offense." In other words, even Jesus' rebuke to Peter is a further wordplay on his name and his calling.[39]

What should we make of this? In a way, Simon can be Simon, the fisherman, without a lived relationship with Christ. True, he won't be able to achieve the fullness of his calling, but he can at least muddle along, and perhaps even achieve some earthly measure of success along the way. But Simon can't become Peter without Christ. Maybe we can imagine Simon, by his own strength and charm, deciding to go from catching fish to "catching men." Certainly, we can envision any number of trades or professions or natural skill sets that might be useful for evangelization or discipleship. But what Christ is revealing to Peter — that he's the rock on whom Christ will build his Church — isn't something Simon can provide for himself.

That's why Jesus praises Simon the first time around, for "flesh and blood has not revealed this to you, but my Father who is in heaven" (Mt 16:17). Simon's ability to understand who Christ is comes from his attentiveness to the voice of the Father. But then Simon Peter decides to protect Jesus from the cross, to save Christ from his destiny and our salvation. It's as if the moment he achieves some measure of growth in the spiritual life, he starts to feel good about himself and immediately falls backward. He is hardly the last Christian to have stumbled in this way. And for this Jesus rebukes him, saying, "You are not on the side of God, but of men" (Mt 16:22–23). And so John Calvin is right, in a sense. With Simon Peter, as with every one of his successors, we find these two traits comingled. As Father Joseph Ratzinger, the future Pope Benedict XVI, remarked, "Has it not remained this way throughout all Church history, that the pope, the successor of Peter, has been *petra* and *skandalon*, rock of God and stumbling stone all in one?"[40] Ratzinger continued:

> If it all depended on Peter, if flesh and blood are speaking from him, then he can be Satan and a stumbling

stone. But if he lets himself be taken completely into service by God, then, as God's instrument, he can really be a cosmic stone. But that is no expression of his achievement and his character but the name of an election and a sending to which no one is competent by nature, least of all this Simon who in his natural character is anything but a rock. That he is the one who is declared to be the rock, that is the fundamental paradox of divine grace which works in weakness.[41]

Although Ratzinger's point is specific to the papacy, there's a broader sense in which it's true of us all. As we're about to see, Jesus invites us to places none of us can get to on our own, in order to become the saints we were created to be — fully, truly ourselves.

You

What do names look like in your life? Chances are, you're not called to become pope, like Simon Peter, or to invent the first proper nouns in a language, like Adam. But you're still someone for whom names are vitally important. Maybe you've spent years "making a name for yourself" in the business world, or trading on (or trying to overcome) your family name. Or maybe you've been told, or even believe, that you need to "invent yourself" or "define yourself." In themselves, those things aren't necessarily good or bad. What they are is incomplete. We live in a world in which people reduce others and even themselves into overly simplistic categories. In lieu of a name-based identity, too many of us have settled for generic group identities: You are your sexual orientation, or your race, or your gender, or your job. And to be sure, each of those things helps to make you who you are, but you're not reducible to any one of them. You're so much more than that.

In the Book of Revelation, Jesus delivers the Holy Spirit's message to the churches: "To him who conquers I will give some of the hidden manna, and I will give him a white stone, with a new name written on the stone which no one knows except him who receives it" (2:17). What is this "hidden manna"? Saint Ambrose (d. 397; the famed bishop of Milan who brought Saint Augustine into the Church) connects the manna, the daily bread of the Jews, to the Christian Eucharist. He describes the Eucharist by saying that the "manna came from heaven, this is above the heavens; that was of heaven, this is of the Lord of the heavens; that was liable to corruption, if kept a second day, this is far from all corruption, for whosoever shall taste it holily shall not be able to feel corruption."[42] It's perhaps the highest expression of divine intimacy imaginable: the idea of a full spiritual and even bodily communion between you and the living God. But we can also say with Saint Francis de Sales (1567–1622) that "prayer is a manna, for the infinity of delicious tastes and precious sweetnesses which it gives to such as use it, but it is hidden, because it falls before the light of any science, in the mental solitude where the soul alone treats with her God alone."[43] Both our reception of the Eucharist and our private prayer ought to be times of true personal intimacy with God — giving ourselves totally to him, in order to receive totally from him. That's the sort of intimacy evoked by the "hidden manna."

The intimacy of the "hidden manna" is coupled with the intimacy of being given a new name, one known only to you and God. Recall that your journey with Christ is one of "a humanization alongside a deification."[44] He is calling you toward something that you cannot achieve on your own, something possible only with his grace. That is, he's calling you to become Godlike, to be able to say, "It is no longer I who live, but Christ who lives in me; and the life I now live in the flesh I live by faith in the Son of God, who loved me and gave himself for me" (Gal 2:20).

Paradoxically, it is precisely in doing this that you will also find yourself most fully becoming yourself. The message of Christianity is not only that you ought to desire truth, goodness, and beauty. It's that you already do. In the language of Saint

Thomas Aquinas, "Good is that which all things seek after," and so the "first precept of law" is that "good is to be done and pursued, and evil is to be avoided."[45] This means two things: both that good is what we *do* seek, and that good is what we *should* seek. The moral law, in the Christian vision of the universe, is not primarily an external set of rules arbitrarily limiting our freedom. Instead, it's more like an instruction guide for our hearts. It's there to help us achieve the good we want, against our constant temptation to self-sabotage and self-destruct. You are inescapably drawn toward these like a moth to light, and you are insatiable in this question, never being content with a little truth, a little goodness, or a little beauty. We can see this most clearly, ironically, in those moments in which we're furthest from goodness. Amazingly, even when we sin, we do so not simply for the sake of sinning, but out of a misguided quest for some real or apparent good.[46] Consider the last serious sin you commit or contemplated. Why did you want to do it? Whatever the motive (be it pleasure, catharsis, the respect of others, or a desire to be known or loved), it can probably be put this way: you wanted a good thing and pursued it in a bad way. It's why Father Smith, the titular character in the Bruce Marshall novel, can say that "the young man who rings the bell at the brothel is unconsciously looking for God."[47]

Sin, in other words, consists in chasing false goods instead of real ones, or lower goods instead of higher ones. As a result, sin can never satisfy. Neither can any other worldly pursuit. You can have all the money, sex, power, fame, glory, and honor that the world can offer and still be left unsatisfied. In an interview with *Sixty Minutes*, New England Patriots quarterback Tom Brady puts it this way:

> Why do I have three Super Bowl rings, and still think there's something greater out there for me? I mean, maybe a lot of people would say, "Hey man, this is what is." I reached my goal, my dream, my life. Me, I think:

God, it's gotta be more than this. I mean this can't be what it's all cracked up to be. I mean I've done it. I'm 27. And what else is there for me?[48]

Brady's interviewer, Steve Kroft, responds, "What's the answer?" to which Brady says, "I wish I knew. I wish I knew." To this, Pope Francis would respond, "Our infinite sadness can only be cured by an infinite love."[49] Or, as Saint Augustine said to God many years ago, "Thou hast formed us for Thyself, and our hearts are restless till they find rest in Thee."[50] We'll return to Augustine, and to this understanding of happiness, in the next chapter.

For now, recognize that all of this means that the pursuit of holiness is deeply humanizing. In fact, it's more than that. Sanctity doesn't just make you more Godlike and more deeply human. It makes you more fully yourself. The great dictators of history have biographies that become tediously monotonous in their similarity. The rise to power, the insatiable hunger for more, more, more, and the ultimate defeat. But the saints, in contrast, are remarkably different one from another. That's one of the things that's beautiful about God's promise in Revelation: each name is distinct. The saints aren't interchangeable. Each is unique. And this isn't true only in heaven. Christ compares his graces to pearls (see Mt 7:6; 13:45–46), and the beautiful thing about pearls isn't just that they're valuable, but that each is beautiful in its own individual way. Pliny the Elder, the first-century Roman author, mentions that the Romans took to calling the pearl *unio*, or "the unique gem," because "no two pearls are ever found perfectly alike."[51] That's how Christ's graces are.[52] It's in this way that Father Luigi Giussani (1922–2005) could say that in the Catholic tradition, the holy person is a saint, and, in the strictest sense of the word, the saint is the individual who realizes more completely his or her own personality, what he or she is supposed to be. The word "holiness" coincides in the total sense with a true personality. If one is self-fulfilled, he is realizing the idea for which he was created. In fact, for the Church, the concept of sin signifies what first of all obstructs an individual from realizing his personality.[53]

This view gets things correct. We indulge in selfishness and sin partly because we're afraid of losing ourselves if we give ourselves to Christ. But if we're made by and for God, then it's *only* in giving ourselves to Christ that we find true self-fulfillment, since it is only in Christ that we can be truly full. As Pope Francis put it, "Holiness does not make you less human, since it is an encounter between your weakness and the power of God's grace."[54] Christ wanted to make Simon more fully Simon, and he wants to make you more fully yourself. This is the first dimension of your name and identity in Christ.

Francis de Sales is credited with the line, "Be who you are and be that perfectly well," and it sounds like the kind of gooey self-help advice you'd find in any number of popular "you can do it!" books.[55] Francis seems to be simply saying that the Simons of the world should be the best fishermen they can possibly be. But Francis's statement holds a great deal more substance and nuance. He knows well that Simons are sometimes called to become Peters. The slightly misquoted line above comes from a letter he wrote to Saint Jane Frances de Chantal (1572–1641).[56] Francis was Jane's friend and spiritual director, and their friendship is no small part of the reason that they each became the saints that they are. Their letters back and forth give us a glimpse of what holy friendship and good spiritual direction look like.

The relevant part of the letter in question begins "Do not love anything too much, I beg you, not even virtues, which we sometimes lose by our excessive zeal." That's a shocking line from a saint, since it sounds as if he's saying not to be too virtuous. Instead, he's saying not to invest your love in achieving this or that virtue. It's a question, he says, of "your desires and your fervor," for "it seems to me that white is not the color proper to roses, for red roses are more beautiful and more fragrant; however, white is the distinctive characteristic of lilies." In other words, we waste so much energy comparing ourselves with others and trying to become the saint someone else is meant to be that it takes us away from the holiness that we're actually called to. Recall the earlier point, that to name a particular animal as a cat is to say that it's not a dog. To say that you're Sarah is to say that you're not Jenny. So, judging yourself by what Jenny is good at or what Jenny is called to is as absurd as judging a cat by how good a dog it is.

Saint Paul puts the matter this way: "For as in one body we have many members, and all the members do not have the same function, so we, though many, are one body in Christ, and individually members one of another" (Rom 12:4–5). The whole Body of Christ is richer because you're *not* the same as the person with whom you're comparing yourself. You're both called in different ways, and you've been given gifts by God. If you become a duplicate of Jenny, you're making yourself redundant, when you should be exercising your unique gifts and talents; this is why Paul immediately proceeds to say that "having gifts that differ according to the grace given to us, let us use them" (Rom 12:6). To fail to live out the particular way that God is calling you to sanctity would be like a nose on the Body of Christ that neglected to smell, because it spent all its time and energy trying to hear. To that nose, Paul says, "If the whole body were an ear, where would be the sense of smell? But as it is, God arranged the organs in the body, each one of them, as he chose" (1 Cor 12:17–18).

As stated above, names help us to place things within our conceptual universe, and our names are one of the means by which we find our place in that universe. Christ calls us by name, he calls us into the lives he has planned for us, but that includes calling us toward a life we can't imagine or foresee. "What no eye has seen, nor ear heard, nor the heart of man conceived, what God has prepared for those who love him," as Saint Paul reminds us in 1 Corinthians 2:9. Our deepest fulfillment will be in the divine intimacy signified by the "hidden manna" of heaven and seeing our truest name, our fullest place in the eternal scheme of things. This idea of being the saint that God calls you to be and made you to be, rather than the saint you want to be, or the saint God called your neighbor to be, is what Francis de Sales is talking about when he says: "Let us be what we are and be that well, in order to bring honor to the Master Craftsman whose handiwork we are. … Let us be what God wants us to be, provided we are His, and let us not be what we would like to be, contrary to His intention. Even if we were the most perfect creatures under heaven, what good would that do us if we were not as God's will would have us be?"[57]

God's promise of a new name is "to him who conquers" (Rv 2:17). And this is what it looks like to conquer: Give yourself over wholly and completely to God, and see the kind of person you become. It might look like God's utilizing the gifts and talents that he has given you that you already recognize, as he did when he called Simon to become a fisher of men. Or it may look like his calling you to something radically new, far outside your comfort zone, to a place where you must constantly rely on his grace, as when he called Simon to become Peter. Either way, hold nothing back, and allow him to make you the kind of saint he wants you to be. That's the saint you were made to be. In doing this, you strive not only to become a clearer image of God, or a more mature child of God; you also strive, whether you know it or not, toward your ultimate divine destiny.

CHAPTER 8

You, and Your Divine Destiny

E ach of the chapters in this book is half of a couplet: Chapter 1 goes with chapter 5, chapter 2 with chapter 6, and so on. The point is that each of the identities of Christ that we've looked at has a sort of "companion identity" within us, and understanding the one helps us to understand the other. But this chapter is coupled with chapter 4, in which we discussed Jesus as Lord and God. What on earth could be our "companion identity" with such a divine claim? As the Lord reminded Saint Catherine of Siena in an apparition to her, "Daughter, thou art she who *is not*. I am He who is."[1] But it turns out, this is only half the story. While we are nothing in comparison with God, this doesn't mean that we're useless or worthless. Rather, God wants to make us like himself, and he has the power to do so. Recognizing this ought to change how we approach the entire question of holiness.

Fire-Insurance Christianity

Why be holy? Why strive to live in the way God calls us to live, particularly given the fact that we don't always feel like living that way, and that God's way is often more difficult (at least in the moment) than our way? Broadly speaking, there are two possible answers. The first is "fire insurance," the idea that Christianity is built chiefly on the doctrine of hell. The idea goes something like this: God has these rules, and if you step out of line, he'll punish you terribly forever. This version of Christianity (and of religion, more broadly) is perhaps most often seen in the writings of atheists describing the way they claim Christians act and the motives behind those actions.

In his book *Atheism: A Brief Insight*, for example, the British humanist Julian Baggini argues that "no matter what is taught in Sunday schools about virtue's own rewards, the threats of punishment, more than promises of rewards even, have been more psychologically effective in getting people to rein in their baser instincts. To believe that God is always watching you and will punish you for any wrongdoing is a very good way of avoiding doing anything contrary to the Church's teachings."[2] Walter Sinnott-Armstrong, in *Morality without God?*, likewise responds to data suggesting that religious people are more generous by arguing that "it seems likely that many religious people donate more to charity than they otherwise would at least partly in order to buy their way into Heaven or buy their way out of Hell," and it's therefore not clear that they deserve any "moral credit" for their good behavior.[3] He concedes that it's unlikely "that many religious people have Heaven and Hell in mind when they help the needy" but suggests that it may still be a subconscious motive.[4] In response to a question about the sexual abuse of children by priests, Richard Dawkins opined that the damage "was arguably less than the long-term psychological damage inflicted by bringing the child up Catholic in the first place."[5] Why? Because of belief in hell, for "if your whole upbringing, and everything you have ever been told by parents, teachers and priests, has led you to believe, *really believe*, utterly and completely, that sinners burn in hell … it is entirely plausible that words could have a more long-lasting and damaging effect than deeds."[6]

If fire insurance faith were the limits of one's exposure to Christianity, it would be easy to imagine our religion as one in which the cowed followers of a fierce god dutifully obey his merciless dictates. Now, it's possible that Dawkins and the other antireligious authors are simply promoting a bit of a straw man, attacking the weakest, most absurd version of Christianity. But for many people, this has been their experience or at least their understanding of Christianity. If so, it's not particularly surprising that they should end up nonbelievers and even disgusted with religion. Such a religion is simply unsustainable, as a person can operate out of a place of fear for only so long before either maturing in his or her faith or collapsing under the strain.

Happiness and Holiness

Fortunately, "fire insurance" is a poor way of understanding Christianity, whether by atheists or by Christians. It simply lacks the power to explain religion seriously. Many Catholics, for example, go to daily Mass. They're not required to, and they're not sinning if they don't. Yet many do. Why? Fire insurance can't explain that away. And so, if we're serious about understanding the question of holiness, we need a deeper answer: the love of God and eternal happiness. A traditional act of contrition (the prayer prayed by the penitent in confession) begins: "O my God, I am heartily sorry for having offended Thee, and I detest all my sins, because I dread the loss of heaven and the pains of hell, but most of all because they offend thee, my God, who art all good and deserving of all my love."[7] Love, not fear, is the chief reason we should seek to turn away from sin and strive for holiness.

You were made for eternal happiness, and you strive continually, whether you know it or not, for that happiness. In 1669, Blaise Pascal noticed: "All men seek happiness. This is without exception. Whatever different means they employ, they all tend to this end. The cause of some going to war and of others avoiding it, is the same desire in both, attended with different views. The will never takes the least step but to this object. This is the motive of every action of every man, even of those who hang themselves."[8] Everything that you do is in pursuit of happiness. But there are higher and lower forms of happiness: the kind that we normally call "joy" versus the kind that only stimulates a rush of pleasure, for example. And some of the things that we think will make us happy don't. Some of the things that make us fleetingly happy make us unhappy in the long run, just as a move in chess might be momentarily satisfying (capturing your opponent's piece, for example) but damaging to your odds of checkmate in the long run. Anyone who has ever overeaten or had too much to drink knows this, and anyone who has seriously engaged in a life of gluttony or drunkenness knows even better. So the question becomes "What sorts of things will make me truly happy, deeply happy, and happy for a long time — even forever?" This is a religious question, but it's also one of the most fundamental questions of human life. To move through life without asking it would be like playing a game without bothering to learn how to win.

The ambition of this book so far has been to shed some light on that question. Some months ago, as a gift for my wife (and not so secretly, for myself), I purchased an espresso machine. After a few months, it began to malfunction. Having no experience with such a machine, I turned to the owner's manual, read online forums about the machine, and even called the manufacturer. The combination of these actions succeeded, and with the necessary fixes in place, my wife and I were back to enjoying homemade lattes. You are dramatically more complicated than that espresso maker, so much so that sometimes you don't understand yourself. Perhaps you can relate to Saint Paul, who said, "I do not understand my own actions. For I do not do what I want, but I do the very thing I hate. ... For I do not do the good I want, but the evil I do not want is what I do" (Rom 7:15, 19).

What should you do when you find yourself malfunctioning? Turn to Scripture, the sort of owner's manual God has given us. Turn to the Church, reaching out to those who may be able to shed some insight into the problems you're facing. Chances are good that, like the problems I had with the espresso maker, someone else has faced — and overcome — whatever you're struggling with. And this community of believers includes that "great cloud of witnesses" (Heb 12:1) who have gone before us. But neither Scripture nor the Church replaces the need for you to talk to your manufacturer, as it were: your Creator. And what do these three have to say in response to the question of how you operate? Namely, that you were made for love, and the higher the love, the happier you are. Therefore, "let us love one another; for love is of God, and he who loves is born of God and knows God" (1 Jn 4:7). The highest and most permanent love is the love of God — to be loved by, and to love, God for all eternity satisfies the human heart in a way that nothing else does. Recall again the immortal words of Saint Augustine, "Thou hast formed us for Thyself, and our hearts are restless till they find rest in Thee."[9]

Understanding that holiness is key to meaningful happiness revolutionizes how we understand sin. The sociologist Gail Dines wrote in the *Washington Post* that it "doesn't matter" whether or not pornography is sinful but that we should still be concerned about it, because science has shown that it negatively impacts "how we think about gender, sexuality, relationships, intimacy, sexual violence and gender equality."[10] But calling something a sin simply expresses that it's something that harms us and others. In the light of our being made for eternal happiness, "sin" is any intentional action by which we choose a lower good over a higher one, or a false good over a real one. It's the spiritual equivalent to driving your car with the handbrake on — it's wrong because it's bad for your car, and if you fully understood what you were doing to the car internally, you would shudder.

A cynic might read this and say, "But that's just a word game — pursuing eternal reward rather than avoiding eternal punishment!" Not so. Imagine that the question was "Why study?" A shallow answer would be "So as not to fail." And it's true that the possibility of failing (like the possibility of hell) does exist. But that's a poor reason to study and is a motivation for only the worst of students. It encourages working only as hard as needed to pass: to aim for the D-minus and to see how much you can get away with. Teachers with this toxic approach to education begin to "teach to the test," focusing less on a well-rounded curriculum and more on the handful of questions likely to be on the standardized testing at the end of the year.[11] Students with this approach to education are unlikely to succeed, and it's no great surprise if the anxious avoidance of failing becomes too much, and they drop out entirely.

Good students and teachers, on the other hand, those who really know why they're in the classroom, are motivated by love of the material. They seek to increase their knowledge of the subject and of the world at large, to expand their intellectual horizons and to enrich their lives. The thought of failing may never cross such students' minds. Students who voluntarily opt for advanced classes, for example, are likely not motivated by fear of failing, but by something more akin to love. And we see something similar to this across many strata of human life: Those who succeed tend to be those motivated by love rather than fear. If you enter marriage asking, "How much can I get away with and not get divorced?" your marriage is already in trouble. If your approach to friendship is to determine how little time you can spend with someone without being cut off entirely, you're unlikely to see that relationship flourish.

So it is with holiness. Those who are struggling in their faith — for example, those tempted to do something seriously immoral, or tempted to abandon faith altogether — may benefit from the reminder that it's possible to fail, that it's possible to end up in hell. But in the lives of those who are growing in their faith, hell plays an ever-diminishing role, as it becomes less of a possibility. Virtually everything said so far in this chapter is encapsulated perfectly in a single verse by Saint John: "There is no fear in love, but perfect love casts out fear. For fear has to do with punishment, and he who fears is not perfected in love" (1 Jn 4:18). As Aquinas notes, the Christian grows from servile fear ("whereby one fears punishment") to what's called filial fear ("whereby a son fears to offend his father or to be separated from him"), so that, the closer a man clings to charity, "the more confident he is of the reward, and, consequently the less fearful of punishment."[12]

This is the reason we strive for holiness: not primarily because we're terrified of failing, but because we're invited to something magnificent and given the grace to achieve it. In the encouraging words of Pope Saint Leo the Great (A.D. 400–461): "Realize, O Christian, your dignity. Once made a partaker in the divine nature, do not return to your former baseness by a life unworthy [of that dignity]. Remember whose head it is and whose body of which you constitute a member."[13] But what is this divine partaking to which Leo refers?

The Divine Promises

We Christians tend to have a much more vivid image of hell than we do of heaven. Billy Graham, in his early days, described heaven this way: "We are going to sit around the fireplace and have parties, and the angels will wait on us, and we'll drive down the golden streets in a yellow Cadillac convertible."[14] He later matured past such a vision, but many of us haven't. Our imagined heavens tend to err in one of either two ways. The first way is to imagine a heaven that's dull and sanctimonious: folks dressed in white sitting on clouds and playing harps. Who would want to strive or sacrifice for such a boring eternity? The second is to imagine heaven in a way that's too carnal. In other words, we put off all the partying and materialism now so that we can have better parties and Cadillacs in heaven. This vision subtly assumes that all of our fleshly pursuits really are what would make us happy if only we could get enough of them.

Saint Paul tells the church at Thessalonica that God called them "from the beginning" to be saved through his preaching, "so that you may obtain the glory of our Lord Jesus Christ" (2 Thes 2:14). So the Christian life is a call to glory, to Christ's glory. Elsewhere, Paul speaks of how he shares "a secret and hidden wisdom of God, which God decreed before the ages for our glorification" (1 Cor 2:7). And here Paul acknowledges the limitations of our understanding of heaven: "What no eye has seen, nor ear heard, nor the heart of man conceived, what God has prepared for those who love him" (1 Cor 2:9). We are better at visualizing hell than heaven because we have some sense of what the suffering of hell is like, but heaven is indescribably glorious.

But fortunately, Paul and the other New Testament writers don't leave it at that. What they depict is so radical that you might be tempted to disbelieve it, and it's a teaching somehow so little preached that you may not even realize it's part of the Gospel. The teaching is, in a word, that we'll be made divine. The *Catechism of the Catholic Church* puts it this way in paragraph 460:

> The Word became flesh to make us "partakers of the divine nature": "For this is why the Word became man, and the Son of God became the Son of man: so that man, by entering into communion with the Word and thus receiving divine sonship, might become a son of God" "For the Son of God became man so that we might become God." "The only-begotten Son of God, wanting to make us sharers in his divinity, assumed our nature, so that he, made man, might make men gods."

This is not just some crazy Catholic belief, akin to the Mormon idea that we become the gods and goddesses of our own universes, each with our own planet.[15] Rather, this is the clear teaching of Jesus, of the apostles, of the earliest Christians, and of 2,000 years of Christianity, as evidenced by the sheer number of quotations within that short paragraph from the *Catechism*.[16]

When Saint Paul speaks of our predestined glorification, he means that "we all, with unveiled face, beholding the glory of the Lord, are being changed into his likeness from one degree of glory to another" (2 Cor 3:18). So, the goal of our becoming ever more glorified, of passing from glory into glory, is to be changed into Christ's likeness. Saint Peter sounds the same note when he speaks of how "his divine power has granted to us all things that pertain to life and godliness, through the knowledge of him who called us to his own glory and excellence, by which he has granted to us his precious and very great promises, that through these you may escape from the corruption that is in the world because of passion, and become partakers of the divine nature" (2 Pt 1:3–4).

The point of the Christian life isn't just to avoid the corruption of the world (still less simply to avoid hell) but to receive the full wealth of life and goodness, to receive Christ's glory and excellence, and ultimately to "become partakers of the divine nature." This path is referred to as "glorification," "theosis," or "divinization," and both Saint Paul and Saint John connect it to the idea of being sons and daughters of God. John puts it this way: "See what love the Father has given us, that we should be called children of God; and so we are. The reason why the world does not know us is that it did not know him. Beloved, we are God's children now; it does not yet appear what we shall be, but we know that when he appears we shall be like him, for we shall see him as he is" (1 Jn 3:1–2).

We're already children of God by baptism, as mind-boggling and incredible as that is, but what God has in store for us is beyond what we can even envision: to become like Christ, to partake of the divine nature. But, by far, the most shocking thing said on the subject of divinization is from Jesus' own lips. When the crowds rose to stone him for blasphemy for calling himself the Son of God, Jesus answered them by pointing out that even the psalm (specifically, Ps 82:6) says, "You are gods, sons of the Most High, all of you." Jesus explicated the verse by saying that the psalmist "called them gods to whom the word of God came" (Jn 10:35).

In saying that we become partakers of the divine nature, that we inherit Christ, that we share in his glory, and become "gods" by receiving the word of God, Scripture is not saying that the saints are gods and goddesses apart from the one true God. Nor are they divine by nature in the way that God is, Saint Athanasius points out that what Scripture says about divinization is really an extension of what it says about being a son or daughter of God: "Although there be one Son by nature, True and Only-begotten, we too become sons, not as He in nature and truth, but according to the grace of Him that calls, and though we are men from the earth, are yet called gods, not as the True God or His Word, but as has pleased God who has given us that grace."[17]

Jesus is the only-begotten Son of the Father, the only Son of the Father by nature. But by grace, he shares that sonship with us, so that we can be sons and daughters of God as well. As we saw in chapter 4, to be a Son of God is to be divine by adoption. Athanasius points out that we see some semblance of this in the moral life. For instance, we "become merciful, not by being made equal to God," but by receiving grace from God and imparting it to others.[18] When Jesus says that "no one is good but God alone" (Lk 18:19), he's reminding us that human goodness is a participation in what is properly God's. A good man isn't good because he has some storehouse of goodness apart from God's goodness. He's good because he is enabled, through grace, to share in the goodness that is properly divine. It's the same story if we talk about how that good man can be called a son of God, and even called a god.

Achieving Glory

Godliness, in other words, is becoming Godlike, and it's something that we can't achieve on our own. But we can achieve it, through the contemplation of Christ. Perhaps you noticed a thread running through the scriptural passages quoted earlier. Paul describes glorification as occurring amid our own "beholding the glory of the Lord" (2 Cor 3:18); Peter describes it as occurring "through the knowledge of him who called us to his own glory and excellence" (2 Pt 1:3); and John says we'll be like him "for we shall see him as he is" (1 Jn 3:2). In other words, each author connects our glorification with our contemplation of Christ. Seeing him changes us, and the more time we spend gazing upon him, the more we become like him. Jesus likewise applies "gods" to those "to whom the word of God came" (Jn 10:35).

Great thinkers such as Aristotle had (apparently simply through the use of reason) realized that the highest, most lasting form of human happiness must be in contemplation, since it is the action closest to divinity. Aristotle observed that "happiness extends indeed just as far as contemplation does, and those to whom it more belongs to contemplate, it also more belongs to be happy, not coincidentally."[19] That was a brilliant realization, but it's limited, because Aristotle lacked any knowledge of grace. His understanding of heaven is man knowing and loving divinity to the best of man's ability.

The problem is clear enough: Even for the most brilliant of men, such as Aristotle, there are radical limitations in both human knowledge and human love. The Christian promise goes further: that we can love God with God's own love. How? "God's love has been poured into our hearts through the Holy Spirit who has been given to us" (Rom 5:5). This is the meaning of Saint Paul's saying: "For now we see in a mirror dimly, but then face to face. Now I know in part; then I shall understand fully, even as I have been fully understood. So faith, hope, love abide, these three; but the greatest of these is love" (1 Cor 13:12–13). In seeing God fully, we shall know and love as he knows and loves, because we will know and love with his own knowledge and love.

And so, as much as possible, we should set our sights always on Jesus Christ. The more time we spend contemplating, conversing with, and emulating him, the more we will become like him. Saint Clare of Assisi (1194–1253), who founded the female branch of the Franciscan Order, reminded one of the sisters under her care that Jesus "is the splendor of eternal glory, the brightness of eternal light, and the mirror without cloud," and advised each one, "Queen and bride of Jesus Christ, look into the mirror daily and study well your reflection, that you may adorn yourself, mind and body, with an enveloping garment of every virtue, and thus find yourself attired in flowers and gowns befitting the daughter and most chaste bride of the king on high."[20]

The more we engage in such contemplation, the more we can see ourselves transformed into Christ. This process isn't completed until our entry into heaven. Saint John of the Cross (1542–1591) writes that "in heaven the will of the soul is not destroyed, it is so intimately united with the power of the will of God, Who loves it, that it loves Him as strongly and as perfectly as it is loved of Him; both wills being united in one sole will and one sole love of God."[21] This is, of course, an imitation of Christ himself. Being both fully human and fully divine, he possesses both a human will and a divine will, yet even his perfect human will was and is in total union with the will of the Father. This is true also of the saints in heaven: their wills are totally free and yet they want only the will of the Father.

We often think of free will in terms of the innate capacity to sin, but this isn't quite right. If it were, we would have to say that God himself doesn't have free will, since he's incapable of acting contrary to his own perfect nature. A better way of understanding free will is to recall the earlier point that our wills *always* seek the good, just as our intellects are insatiable for knowing the truth. We pursue truth and goodness quite imperfectly, deluding ourselves into thinking we'll be happy in settling for something less than the full truth or the highest good. In heaven, we can't desire anything other than the will of God for the same reason that a person who knows the full truth of a situation can't fall for a lie about it; the intellect and the will are beyond error. We can't be fully satisfied until we achieve the fullness of truth and goodness, yet we can't achieve this fullness on our own. This is one reason we draw near to Christ, who can raise us to these levels of divine knowledge and love.

Tied to this, from a Catholic perspective, are the unique roles of the Mass and Eucharistic adoration. The more time we spend before Jesus, open to what he wants to do for (and to) us, the more we'll grow to be like him and to desire his will. And so, we should make spending time in his presence in the Eucharist a priority. Christ promises that "if any one eats of this bread, he will live for ever; and the bread which I shall give for the life of the world is my flesh" (Jn 6:51). A joint Catholic-Orthodox statement notes that "by the communion in the body and blood of Christ, the faithful grow in that mystical divinization which makes them dwell in the Son and the Father, through the Spirit."[22] There, in an intimate and unique way, believers encounter Christ. As Saint John Chrysostom, in his great work *On the Priesthood*, describes it:

> For the priestly office is indeed discharged on earth, but it ranks among heavenly ordinances; and very naturally so: for neither man, nor angel, nor archangel, nor any other created power, but the Paraclete Himself, instituted this vocation, and persuaded men while still abiding in the flesh to represent the ministry of angels. ...
>
> For when you see the Lord sacrificed, and laid upon the altar, and the priest standing and praying over the victim, and all the worshippers empurpled with that precious blood, can you then think that you are still among men, and standing upon the earth? Are you not, on the contrary, straightway translated to Heaven, and casting out every carnal thought from the soul, do you not with disembodied spirit and pure reason contemplate the things which are in Heaven? Oh! What a marvel! What love of God to man! He who sits on high with the Father is at that hour held in the hands of all, and gives Himself to those who are willing to embrace and grasp Him. And this all do through the eyes of faith![23]

Most of our other acts of prayer and worship are man-made, a matter of our reaching out to God. But in the case of the Eucharistic Sacrifice, instituted by Christ at the Last Supper (Lk 22:19), we see God reaching out toward us and inviting us into something above us. Our time in the presence of the Blessed Sacrament, particularly in the liturgical context of the Mass, is the nearest thing we get to heaven while here on earth. Therefore, we should prioritize this, if we seriously believe what Scripture says about how we become divinized.

Suffering and Divinization

This is not to suggest that it's only in set-aside times of worship that we become conformed to Christ. As Pope Francis has said, "Each saint is a mission, planned by the Father to reflect and embody, at a specific moment in history, a certain aspect of the Gospel." This entails that "holiness is experiencing, in union with Christ, the mysteries of his life," both in "uniting ourselves to the Lord's death and resurrection in a unique and personal way" and "reproducing in our own lives various aspects of Jesus' earthly life: his hidden life, his life in community, his closeness to the outcast, his poverty and other ways in which he showed his self-sacrificing love."[24] That is, each moment of our lives can be spiritually united with Christ.

For instance, when we are persecuted and bear it graciously, we come to a deeper understanding of Christ's sufferings. In showing mercy to others, or experiencing their mercy, we learn a bit more about God's mercy toward us. Saint Paul describes this kind of Christ-united life by saying, "I have been crucified with Christ; it is no longer I who live, but Christ who lives in me; and the life I now live in the flesh I live by faith in the Son of God, who loved me and gave himself for me" (Gal 2:20). Instead of waiting for heaven, we ought even now to live in such a way that we can say the same.

This is particularly true in our times of suffering. Hebrews speaks of Jesus as "crowned with glory and honor because of the suffering of death" and inviting us to join him in the same; that "in bringing many sons to glory," God should "make the pioneer of their salvation perfect through suffering" (Heb 2:9–10). Likewise, Saint Paul says to the Romans that we are heirs of Christ if "we suffer with him in order that we may also be glorified with him" (Rom 8:17). If we unite our sufferings to Christ on the cross, he will see us through them and will lead us from the cross of Good Friday to the glory of Easter.

The Weight of Glory

Up to this point, we've considered primarily you and your divine destiny. But your destiny is also your neighbor's destiny, and you should respect him accordingly. C. S. Lewis remarked that it may be possible for a man "to think too much of his own potential glory hereafter; it is hardly possible to think too often or too deeply about that of his neighbor."[25] He concludes by saying:

> It is a serious thing to live in a society of possible gods and goddesses, to remember that the dullest and most uninteresting person you talk to may one day be a creature which, if you saw it now, you would be strongly tempted to worship, or else a horror and a corruption such as you now meet, if at all, only in a nightmare. All day long we are, in some degree, helping each other to one or other of these destinations. It is in the light of these overwhelming possibilities, it is with the awe and the circumspection proper to them, that we should conduct all our dealings with one another, all friendships, all loves, all play, all politics.
>
> There are no *ordinary* people. You have never talked to a mere mortal. Nations, cultures, arts, civilization — these are mortal, and their life is to ours as the life of a gnat. But it is immortals whom we joke with, work with, marry, snub, and exploit — immortal horrors or everlasting splendours. ... Next to the Blessed Sacrament itself, your neighbour is the holiest object presented to your senses. If he is your Christian neighbour he is holy in almost the same way, for in him also Christ *vere*

> *latitat* — the glorifier and the glorified, Glory Himself,
> is truly hidden.[26]

Recall the line (examined in chapter 5) "If any one says, 'I love God,' and hates his brother, he is a liar; for he who does not love his brother whom he has seen, cannot love God whom he has not seen" (1 Jn 4:20). In loving your brother, you're honoring that which is most Godlike in the visible world. If you're dating someone with kids, and you hate his kids, the relationship probably isn't going to go very far. Nor should it. Likewise, you can't love God while hating his children. If you know who God is, who you are, and who your neighbor is, you should approach your neighbor with love and even a certain sense of awe. Love neighbor, love God, and be prepared for love to transform you into your divine destiny.

Conclusion

Who Will You Be?

In psychology (and in many other social sciences), the "observer effect" refers to "changes in a subject's behavior caused by an awareness of being observed."[1] The mere presence of a researcher can corrupt data, because humans (and even animals) behave differently when they know they're being watched. For instance, in what's called the "human shield effect," animals that ordinarily are vigilant in keeping an eye out for predators tend to relax when they know that nonthreatening human observers are around.[2] We find something similar in quantum physics, strangely enough. Particles, it turns out, behave similarly toward animals and humans, with experiments showing that "the greater the amount of 'watching,' the greater the observer's influence on what actually takes place" even at the level of particles.[3]

In other words, it's easy to think of observation as a merely passive thing. Think of Ebenezer Scrooge in *A Christmas Carol*, helplessly observing his past, present, and future self. But the Gospel isn't like that at all. An encounter with the Gospel is more like Scrooge at the end of the play: having seen all of this, we must now either change our lives or carry on as before. But even if we choose to carry on, things have changed. Once we begin to plumb the depths of the Christian Gospel, we can no longer go back to our previous, ignorant state. Saint Paul, summarizing the Roman Empire's pre-Christian pagan history, told the Athenians that "the times of ignorance God overlooked, but now he commands all men everywhere to repent" (Acts 17:30). In other words, a decision is now required to accept or to reject the Gospel, to accept or to reject Christ. There's no longer an option for ignorance or neutrality.

Divine contemplation likewise changes things, especially for the people doing the contemplating. This sort of contemplation is what eternal life is made of, as we learn from Jesus' prayer at the Last Supper, in which he says, "And this is eternal life, that they know you the only true God, and Jesus Christ whom you have sent" (Jn 17:3).

Aquinas points out that no one comprehends God, in the sense of understanding him completely and perfectly, not even the saints and angels in heaven.[4] Our sinfulness and God's hiddenness, as well as the inherent limitations of the finitude of our intellects and our wills, keep us from knowing him thoroughly. Our minds and hearts are satiated in God, but not in a way that exhausts him. He's always more than we can grasp. One happy consequence of this is that, just as "star differs from star in glory" (1 Cor 15:41), the saints and angels in heaven differ in glory, related to the degree to which they know and love God. For what other standard could possibly matter in the scheme of things?

As a girl, Saint Thérèse of Lisieux (1873–1897) struggled to grasp this reality. How could God give unequal amounts of glory to the elect in heaven? Wouldn't that mean that some people would go through eternity in heaven discontented? Her sister Pauline responded with a brilliant demonstration, filling a large tumbler and a small thimble to the brim. Which one, Pauline asked, was fuller? "I told her each was as full as the other and that it was impossible to put in more water than they could contain," Thérèse would later recall, and she thus came to "understand that in heaven God will grant His Elect as much glory as they can take, the last having nothing to envy in the first."[5] The good news is that we can grow from a thimble to a tumbler.

How? By desiring God. Saint Augustine describes it as a sort of spiritual "stretching":

> The whole life of a good Christian is a holy longing. But what you long for you do not yet see, but by longing you are made capacious so that when what you are to see has come, you may be filled. For just as, if you should wish to fill a pocket, and you know how big the object that will be put in is, you stretch the pocket, whether made of sackcloth or leather or any thing — you know how large a thing you will place there, and you see that the pocket is narrow. By stretching you make it more capacious. So God, by postponing, stretches the longing, by longing stretches the soul, by stretching makes it capacious. Let us long, therefore, brothers, because we are going to be filled.[6]

We worry that God isn't going to be enough to fill our hearts, and so we try to supplement by adding glory, and money, and fame, and sex, and booze, and feasting, and the rest. But the truth is, our hearts aren't too big for God to fill. Our hearts are too small. We should want to have our hearts stretched for the same reason that people might skip lunch and appetizers when they're anticipating a particularly succulent dinner.

This is the truth underlying the book you've been reading. The more time you spend in loving contemplation of Jesus Christ, and the more you're open to his vision of your identity, the more you'll be "transformed by the renewal of your mind" (Rom 12:2). Slowly but surely, you will find the pocket of your heart expanding from the size of a thimble to the size of a tumbler, as you pass "from one degree of glory to another" (2 Cor 3:18). And then one day, God will pour his love in, in "good measure, pressed down, shaken together, running over" (Lk 6:38), giving you as much glory as you can take.

Acknowledgments

This book was a labor of love, and I have many people to thank for sharing the labor with me. Although I cannot hope to thank everyone who contributed to this book's coming to be, a few people warrant a particular expression of my gratitude. First and foremost, to my wife, Anna, for reading and editing the first drafts of these chapters (often in the middle of the night, when I would complete them), and for encouraging me to write, rather than get distracted by crossword puzzles.

To my parents, Paul and Barbara, for being the first teachers of the faith and for instilling in me the importance of finding my identity in Christ.

To Father Andrew Strobl, for saving my soul in college.

To the FOCUS missionaries and the team at the St. Lawrence Center in Lawrence, Kansas. It was our Bible studies in the fall of 2017 that planted the seed that became this book.

To Simone Rizkallah, with whom I discussed these ideas as I prepared for the Bible studies.

To Brandon Vogt, David Bates, and everyone else who encouraged me to write a book, and not just talk about it for years.

To Mary Beth, Rebecca, and the whole team at Our Sunday Visitor for taking a chance on me as a first-time author, and for turning the raw materials I provided into a book.

And to my beautiful daughter, Stella Maris, for being two weeks late in being born, giving me time to finalize the manuscript and to reflect in a fresh way on the importance of naming.

Notes

Introduction

1. Matthew Gault, "Sebastian Junger Knows Why Young Men Go to War," *War Is Boring*, January 28, 2015, accessed December 3, 2019, https://medium.com/war-is-boring/sebastian-junger-knows-why-young-men-go-to-war-f163804cbf6.
2. Adam Linehan, "Sebastian Junger: Over-Valorizing Vets Does More Harm Than Good," *Task and Purpose*, May 24, 2016, accessed December 3, 2019, https://taskandpurpose.com/sebastian-junger-we-need-to-stop-over-valorizing-veterans.
3. John Paul II, *Fides et Ratio*, accessed December 3, 2019, Vatican.va, par. 1.
4. Gault, "Sebastian Junger Knows."
5. Gemma Strong, "Why Kate Is Forbidden from Signing Autographs for Fans," *Hello! Magazine*, December 5, 2017, accessed December 3, 2019, https://www.hellomagazine.com/royalty/2017120544532/why-kate-middleton-cant-sign-autographs/.
6. Ruby Buddemeyer, "50 Strict Rules the Royal Family Has to Follow," *Marie Claire*, August 25, 2017, accessed December 3, 2019, https://www.marieclaire.com/culture/g4985/strict-rules-the-royal-family-has-to-follow/.
7. In the case of the signature ban, to minimize the likelihood of someone's forging the royals' signature, and in the case of the dinner protocol, to minimize the risk of someone's feeling

neglected by the queen.

8. Charles Darwin, *The Descent of Man and Selection in Relation to Sex*, 2nd ed. (New York: D. Appleton and Company, 1901), 21.

9. Duke University Medical Center, "Evolution of the Human Appendix: A Biological 'Remnant' No More," *ScienceDaily*, August 21, 2009, accessed December 3, 2019, https://www.sciencedaily.com/releases/2009/08/090820175901.htm.

10. Jerry A. Coyne, *Why Evolution Is True* (Oxford, UK: Oxford University Press, 2009), 65.

11. Jennifer Warner, "Appendix May Actually Have a Purpose," WebMD, October 12, 2007, accessed December 3, 2019, https://www.webmd.com/digestive-disorders/news/20071012/appendix-may-have-purpose. Cf. H. F. Smith, R. E. Fisher, M. L. Everett, A. D. Thomas, R. Randal Bollinger, and W. Parker, "Comparative Anatomy and Phylogenetic Distribution of the Mammalian Cecal Appendix," *Journal of Evolutionary Biology* 22, no. 10 (October 2009): 1984–99.

12. Norman Swan, "The Appendix — Darwin's Mistake," *Cosmos* 67 (February–March 2016), accessed December 3, 2019, https://cosmosmagazine.com/biology/appendix-darwin-s-mistake.

13. Coyne admits that the coccyx has an important function in the human body, as "some useful muscles are attached to it," but still tries to argue that it's vestigial, not because of "its usefulness but because it no longer has the function for which it originally evolved." This argument is circular, however, since it assumes the very thing it sets out to prove (that the human tailbone is simply an evolutionary leftover from an earlier age in which we had tails). Coyne, *Why Evolution Is True*, 66.

14. Richard Dawkins, *River out of Eden: A Darwinian View of Life* (New York: Basic Books, 1995), 133.

15. Coyne, *Why Evolution Is True*, 86.

16. Allen Drury, "Arthur Miller Admits Helping Commu-

nist-Front Groups in '40s," *New York Times*, June 22, 1956, accessed December 3, 2019, http://movies2.nytimes.com/books/00/11/12/specials/miller-front.html.

17. Andrew Glass, "Arthur Miller Testifies before HUAC, June 21, 1956," *Politico*, June 21, 2013, accessed December 3, 2019, https://www.politico.com/story/2013/06/this-day-in-politics-093127.

18. Paul Kengor, "Arthur Miller — Communist," *American Spectator*, October 16, 2015, accessed December 3, 2019, https://spectator.org/64379_arthur-miller-communist/.

19. Arthur Miller, "Why I Wrote 'The Crucible,' " *New Yorker*, October 21, 1996, accessed December 3, 2019, https://www.newyorker.com/magazine/1996/10/21/why-i-wrote-the-crucible.

20. Flannery O'Connor, "To a Professor of English (28 March 61)," in *A Good Man Is Hard to Find*, ed. Frederick Asals (New Brunswick, NJ: Rutgers University Press, 1993), 62–63.

21. Will Oremus, "Here Are All the Different Genders You Can Be on Facebook," *Slate*, February 13, 2014, accessed December 3, 2019, https://slate.com/technology/2014/02/facebook-custom-gender-options-here-are-all-56-custom-options.html.

22. Rhiannon Williams, "Facebook's 71 Gender Options Come to UK Users," *Telegraph*, June 27, 2014, accessed December 3, 2019, https://www.telegraph.co.uk/technology/facebook/10930654/Facebooks-71-gender-options-come-to-UK-users.html.

23. "Facebook Diversity," Facebook, February 26, 2015, accessed December 3, 2019, https://www.facebook.com/facebookdiversity/posts/774221582674346.

24. Francis Fukuyama, "Against Identity Politics," *Foreign Affairs* 97, no. 5 (September–October 2018), accessed December 3, 2019, https://www.foreignaffairs.com/articles/americas/2018-08-14/against-identity-politics-tribalism-francis-fukuyama. Critics of Fukuyama point out that earlier

political movements did the same thing (as one obvious example, the Ku Klux Klan was certainly involved in white "identity politics").

25. Combahee River Collective Statement, quoted in Marianne DeKoven, *Utopia Limited: The Sixties and the Emergence of the Postmodern* (Durham, NC: Duke University Press, 2004), 250. Cf. Keeanga-Yamahtta Taylor, ed., *How We Get Free: Black Feminism and the Combahee River Collective* (Chicago: Haymarket Books, 2017).

26. Sheri Berman, "Why Identity Politics Benefits the Right More Than the Left," *The Guardian*, July 14, 2018, accessed December 3, 2019, https://www.theguardian.com /commentisfree/2018/jul/14/identity-politics-right-left -trump-racism.

27. Jo-Ann Krestan and Claudia Bepko, "Codependency: The Social Reconstruction of Female Experience," in *Feminism and Addiction*, ed. Claudia Bepko (New York: Routledge, 1991), 50.

28. Catherine Ann Cameron and Arantxa Mascarenas, "Digital Social Media in Adolescents' Negotiating Real Virtual Romantic Relationships," in *The Psychology and Dynamics behind Social Media Interactions*, ed. Malinda Desjarlais (Hershey, PA: IGI Global, 2019), 86.

29. Maureen Callahan, "Eat, Pray, Loathe," *New York Post*, December 23, 2007, accessed December 3, 2019, https:// nypost.com/2007/12/23/eat-pray-loathe/.

30. Eric Dean Wilson, "Regarding Diptychs," *American Reader*, September 2014, accessed December 3, 2019, http:// theamericanreader.com/regarding-diptychs/.

31. Some (including the Met's own website) have suggested that this was originally a triptych (the third panel of which is supposedly missing), but this is unlikely. The best evidence suggests that this was originally designed as the diptych we have today. "In the nineteenth century, these panels flanked an *Adoration of the Magi*, now lost, but the frames suggest

that they originally formed a diptych." Bernhard Ridderbos, "Objects and Questions," in *Early Netherlandish Paintings: Rediscovery, Reception and Research*, ed. Bernhard Ridderbos, Anne van Buren, and Henk van Veen, trans. Andrew McCormick and Anne van Buren (Amsterdam: Amsterdam University Press, 2005), 78. Cf. Dagmar Eichberg, *Bildkonzeption and Weltdeutung im New Yorker Diptychon des Jan van Eyck* (Wiesbaden: Dr. Ludwig Reichert Verlag, 1987), 113; Lynn F. Jacobs, *Opening Doors: The Early Netherlandish Triptych Reinterpreted* (University Park, PA: Pennsylvania State University Press, 2012), 300.

32. Francis de Sales, *Introduction to the Devout Life* (London: Rivingtons, 1869), 247.

Chapter 1

1. *The Clear Quran,* trans. Mustafa Khattab (Lombard, IL: Book of Signs Foundation, 2016).
2. Bishop Robert Barron, "Why It Matters Who Jesus Is," *National Catholic Register,* March 14, 2017 (emphasis in original).
3. Bishop Robert Barron, *Catholicism: A Journey to the Heart of the Faith* (New York: Image, 2011), 120–21.
4. Anselm of Canterbury, *Proslogion: With the Replies of Gaunilo and Anselm,* trans. Thomas Williams (Indianapolis, IN: Hackett Publishing, 2011), 7.
5. E.g., Julian Baggini and Gareth Southwell, *Philosophy: Key Themes,* 2nd ed. (Basingstoke, UK: Palgrave Macmillan, 2012), 131.
6. Lyall Watson, quoted in Thomas A. Regelski, *The Bowling Green State University Symposium on Music Teaching and Research* (Bowling Green, OH: Bowling Green State University, 1980), 9.
7. Quoted by his son (and fellow physicist) George Edgin Pugh in *The Biological Origin of Human Values* (New York: Basic Books, 1977), 154.

8. St. Thomas Aquinas, *Commentary on the Book of Causes,* trans. Vincent A. Guagliardo, OP, Charles R. Hess, OP, and Richard C. Taylor (Washington, D.C.: Catholic University of America Press, 1996), proposition 7, 55.

9. See William J. Bodziak, *Footwear Impression Evidence: Detection, Recovery, and Examination,* 2nd ed. (Boca Raton, FL: CRRC Press, 2000).

10. Aquinas, *Commentary on the Book of Causes,* proposition 12, 90.

11. In C. S. Lewis's satirical *Screwtape Letters,* an older demon counsels a young one to encourage this tendency in humans: "Your business is to fix his attention on the stream [of immediate sense experiences]. Teach him to call it 'real life' and don't let him ask what he means by 'real.' " *The Screwtape Letters* (New York: HarperOne, 2001), 2.

12. Steven Pinker, *Where God and Science Meet,* vol. 1, ed. Patrick McNamara (Westport, CT: Praeger Perspectives, 2006), 1, 8.

13. Yiyang Wu, "No Scientific Evidence for God," *Harvard Crimson,* April 21, 2004.

14. There are those who deny this "hardwiring" for God. For example, Phil Zuckerman, a professor of sociology and secular studies, argues against the religious hardwiring because polls show that millions of Americans self-describe as atheist or agnostic, and "the percentage of Americans who claim 'none' as their religion has doubled in recent years." Phil Zuckerman, "Are We 'Hard-Wired' for God?," *Huffington Post,* March 18, 2010, accessed December 3, 2019, https://www.huffpost.com /entry/are-we-hard-wired-for-god_b_411089. What he doesn't mention is that 20 percent of these American "nones" report praying daily, and 27 percent say that they believe in God with "absolute certainty," making them statistically more religious than Western European Christians. Sigal Samuel, "Atheists Are Sometimes More Religious Than Christians," *The Atlantic,* May 31, 2018, accessed December 3, 2019, https://www.theatlantic

.com/international/archive/2018/05/american-atheists
-religious-european-christians/560936/. In any case, the existence of even genuine atheists doesn't disprove our biological
hardwiring for God, any more than the existence of celibates,
single people, homosexuals, and childless couples disproves
our biological hardwiring for procreation. The number of
atheists is surely lower than the number of people who contra-
cept, and yet no one would conclude from the fact of contra-
ception that there isn't an innate biological urge to procreate:
It's just an urge that modern man has found a way of stifling.
For those acquainted with the neuroscience, the question is
not whether we're hardwired for God. Rather, it is whether
our brain is hardwired to *produce* God or to *perceive* God. See
Alexander A. Fingelkurts and Andrew A. Fingelkurts, "Is Our
Brain Hardwired to Produce God, or Is Our Brain Hardwired
to Perceive God? A Systematic Review on the Role of the Brain
in Mediating Religious Experience," *Cognitive Processing* 10,
no. 4 (November 2009): 293–326. The answer to that question
lies outside of neuroscience. For now, it is enough to say that
within man, we find a natural yearning for, and some sense of,
God.

15. Nancy Kanwisher, Josh McDermott, and Marvin M. Chun,
"The Fusiform Face Area: A Module in Human Extrastriate
Cortex Specialized for Face Perception," *Journal of Neuroscience* 17, no. 11 (June 1, 1997): 4302–11, accessed December 3,
2019, https://doi.org/10.1523/JNEUROSCI.17-11-04302.1997.

16. Susan Pinker, *The Village Effect: How Face-to-Face Contact
Can Make Us Healthier and Happier* (Toronto: Random House
Canada, 2014), 289.

17. Masaharu Kato and Ryoko Mugitani, "Pareidolia in Infants," *PLoS ONE* 10, no. 2 (February, 2015), accessed December 3, 2019, https://doi.org/10.1371/journal.pone.0118539.

18. Athanasius of Alexandria, *On the Incarnation*, trans. Sister
Penelope Lawson ("A Religious of C.S.M.V.") (n.p.: Readaclas-
sic.com, 2010), 19.

19. Francis, *Misericordiae Vultus*, accessed December 3, 2019, Vatican.va., par. 1.

20. Athanasius, *On the Incarnation*, 52.

21. Ibid., 21.

22. John Damascene, *On Holy Images*, trans. Mary H. Allies (London: Thomas Baker, 1898), 10 (emphasis added).

23. Ibid.

24. *Sermons of St. Bernard on Advent and Christmas* (London: R. and T. Washbourne, 1909), 72.

25. Kurt Vonnegut, *God Bless You, Dr. Kevorkian* (New York: Washington Square Press, 1999), 9–10.

26. This is largely due to the Protestant Reformation but may also be due in part to the cultural shift brought about with the printing press.

27. Telford Work, *Living and Active: Scripture in the Economy of Salvation* (Grand Rapids, MI: Wm. B. Eerdmans, 2002), xiv.

28. Ibid., 44 (emphasis in original).

29. Ibid., xivn2.

30. Benedict XVI, *Deus Caritas Est*, accessed December 3, 2019, Vatican.va, par. 1.

31. See, e.g., Stephen Arterburn and Jack Felton, *More Jesus, Less Religion: Moving from Rules to Relationship* (Colorado Springs, CO: WaterBrook Press, 2010).

32. Cameron Buettel, "Christianity Is Not a Religion, It's a Relationship," *Grace to You* (blog), February 8, 2016, accessed December 3, 2019, https://www.gty.org/library/blog/B160208/christianity-is-not-a-religion-its-a-relationship (emphasis in original).

33. Nadine DeNinno, " 'Why I Hate Religion but Love Jesus': Controversial YouTube Video Goes Viral," *International Business Times*, January 13, 2012, accessed December 3, 2019, https://www.ibtimes.com/why-i-hate-religion-love-jesus-controversial-youtube-video-goes-viral-395106.

34. Leo Tolstoy, *The Death of Ivan Ilyich*, trans. Richard Pevear and Larissa Volokhonsky (New York: Vintage Classics, 2012), 50.

35. Andrew Stark, *The Consolations of Mortality: Making Sense of Death* (New Haven, CT: Yale University Press, 2016), 15.
36. Ibid., 16.
37. Nicholas Kristof, "Reverend, You Say the Virgin Birth Is 'a Bizarre Claim'?," *New York Times*, April 20, 2019, accessed December 3, 2019, https://www.nytimes.com/2019/04/20/opinion/sunday/christian-easter-serene-jones.html.
38. Quoted in *Days of the Lord: The Liturgical Year*, vol. 1, ed. Robert Gantoy and Romain Swaeles, trans. Gregory LaNave and Donald Molloy (Collegeville, MN: Liturgical Press, 1991), 63–64.
39. One of the chief ways that God manifested himself to the Israelites in their Exodus was through the manna, the "bread from heaven" (Ex 16:4). This prefigured Jesus (Jn 6:51), particularly in his presence in the Eucharist (1 Cor 10:3, 16). Nevertheless, Saint Paul warns that "with most of [the Israelites] God was not pleased; for they were overthrown in the wilderness," and "these things are warnings for us" (1 Cor 10:5–6). They failed to recognize God's presence among them, just as we do today. "For any one who eats and drinks without discerning the body eats and drinks judgment upon himself" (1 Cor 11:29). A recent Pew Research Study found that "just one-third of U.S. Catholics agree" with their Church that the Eucharist is the Body and Blood of Christ and that "most Catholics who believe that the bread and wine are symbolic do not know that the church holds that transubstantiation occurs." Gregory A. Smith, "Just One-Third of U.S. Catholics Agree with Their Church That Eucharist Is Body, Blood of Christ," Pew Research Center, August 5, 2019, accessed December 3, 2019, https://www.pewresearch.org/fact-tank/2019/08/05/transubstantiation-eucharist-u-s-catholics/.

Chapter 2

1. Ann Hornaday, *Talking Pictures: How to Watch Movies* (New

York: Basic Books, 2017), 4.

2. N. M. Kelby, "From Idea to Page in Four Simple Steps," in *The Complete Handbook of Novel Writing: Everything You Need to Know to Create and Sell Your Work*, 3rd ed. (Cincinnati: Writer's Digest Books, 2016), 10.

3. Joseph F. Kelly, *The Origins of Christmas* (Collegeville, MN: Liturgical Press, 2014), 11–12.

4. Matthew likewise connects the two events, but this is less surprising, in that the temptation in the desert (Mt 4:1–11) appears immediately after the baptism in the Jordan (Mt 3:13–17).

5. F. J. Sheed, *To Know Christ Jesus* (Mansfield Centre, CT: Martino Publishing, 2016), 104 (emphasis in original).

6. See William Barclay, *The Daily Study Bible*, vol. 1, *The Gospel of Matthew* (Louisville, KY: Westminster John Knox Press, 2001), 72.

7. This is the order in Matthew's Gospel. Luke reverses the order of the second and third temptations, placing the temptation at the pinnacle of the Temple *after* the temptation in which the Devil "showed him all the kingdoms of the world in a moment of time" (Lk 4:5). Luke seems to be "correcting" Satan here, by placing the Temple in Jerusalem as superior to the whole world. This also fits the broader Lucan theme of Jesus' journey toward Jerusalem (representing Calvary, and his Passion and Resurrection). Thus, we hear that "when the days drew near for him to be received up, he set his face to go to Jerusalem" (9:51), and Jesus explains to the Pharisees that "it cannot be that a prophet should perish away from Jerusalem" (13:33), and more fully to the Apostles: "Behold, we are going up to Jerusalem, and everything that is written of the Son of man by the prophets will be accomplished. For he will be delivered to the Gentiles, and will be mocked and shamefully treated and spit upon; they will scourge him and kill him, and on the third day he will rise" (18:31–33). By reordering the temptations, Luke is placing them on a "journey toward

Jerusalem" of their own.

8. Conditioned as we are to view Christianity as a "religion of the book," we tend to interpret Jesus' words as a biblical mandate to read Scripture. The context of Deuteronomy shows it's actually about the manna, which, in turn, prefigures Jesus himself. For more, see Joe Heschmeyer, "Can You Eat the Word of God?," *Catholic Answers*, October 5, 2018.

9. Sheed, *To Know Christ Jesus*, 108.

10. Kelly, *The Origins of Christmas*, 12.

11. Gregory Rodriguez, "How Genealogy Became Almost as Popular as Porn," *Time*, May 30, 2014, accessed December 3, 2019, http://time.com/133811/how-genealogy-became -almost-as-popular-as-porn/.

12. See Charles Lee Irons, "A Lexical Defense of the Johannine 'Only Begotten,' " in *Retrieving Eternal Generation*, ed. Fred Sanders and Scott R. Swain (Grand Rapids, MI: Zondervan, 2017), 98–116.

13. "Joseph Engelberger," in *Engineers: From the Great Pyramids to the Pioneers of Space Travel*, ed. Adam Hart-Davis (New York: DK Publishing, 2012), 238.

14. Lisa Rogak, *One Big Happy Family: Heartwarming Stories of Animals Caring for One Another* (New York: Thomas Dunne Books, 2013), 75.

15. See Michael F. Bird, *Jesus the Eternal Son: Answering Adoptionist Christology* (Grand Rapids, MI: William B. Eerdmans, 2017).

16. Thomas Keightley, *The Mythology of Ancient Greece and Italy*, 3rd ed. (New York: D. Appleton, 1878), 378.

17. Apollodorus, *The Library*, bk. 3, chap. 9, trans. Robin Hard (Oxford, UK: Oxford University Press, 1997), 115.

18. Arthur Peacocke, *Theology for a Scientific Age: Being and Becoming — Natural, Divine, and Human* (Minneapolis: Fortress Press, 1993), 276.

19. Sheed, *To Know Christ Jesus*, 224 (emphasis in original).

20. Fourth Lateran Council (1215), quoted in Oliver D. Crisp,

The Word Enfleshed: Exploring the Person and Work of Christ (Grand Rapids, MI: Baker Academic, 2016), 4.

Chapter 3

1. Herman Melville, *Moby Dick* (Boston: St. Botolph Society, 1892), 7.
2. "100 Best First Lines from Novels," *American Book Review*, accessed December 3, 2019, http://americanbookreview .org/100BestLines.asp.
3. William Goldman, *The Princess Bride* (Orlando, FL: Harcourt, 2007), 319.
4. William Shakespeare, *Romeo and Juliet* (London: J. Pattie, 1839), 22.
5. Dennis J. McCarthy, "Exod. 3:14: History, Philology, and Theology," *Catholic Biblical Quarterly* 40, no. 3 (July 1978): 315–16.
6. "Names of God," in *The Jewish Encyclopedia,* vol. 9 (New York: Funk and Wagnalls, 1916), 160.
7. McCarthy, "Exod. 3:14," 313.
8. "Nature proceeds little by little from things lifeless to animal life in such a way that it is impossible to determine the exact line of demarcation, nor on which side thereof an intermediate form should lie. Thus, next after lifeless things in the upward scale comes the plant, and of plants one will differ from another as to its amount of apparent vitality; and, in a word, the whole genus of plants, whilst it is devoid of life as compared with an animal, is endowed with life as compared with other corporeal entities. Indeed, as we just remarked, there is observed in plants a continuous scale of ascent towards the animal. So, in the sea, there are certain objects concerning which one would be at a loss to determine whether they be animal or vegetable." Aristotle, *Historia Animalium* [*History of Animals*], trans. D'Arcy Wentworth Thompson, in *The Works of Aristotle*, vol. 4, ed. J. A. Smith and W. D. Ross (Oxford, England: Clar-

endon Press, 1910), 588. In *De Anima* [*On the Soul*], Aristotle
similarly compares and contrasts humans, animals, and plants.
9. Anselm of Canterbury, *Proslogion: With the Replies of
Gaunilo and Anselm*, trans. Thomas Williams (Indianapolis,
IN: Hackett Publishing, 2011), 7. While noting that biblical scholars "would want to find more in the revelation of
the divine name than simply metaphysics," Aidan Nichols,
OP, argues that "it is hard to deny that the biblical author is
making some kind of statement about the God of the Fathers
as a unique referent of the language of being." Aidan Nichols,
Discovering Aquinas (London: Darton, Longman, and Todd,
2002), 43.
10. E. C. B. MacLaurin, "YHWH, the Origin of the Tetragrammaton," *Vetus Testamentum* 12, no. 4 (October 1962): 440.
11. McCarthy, "Exod. 3:14," 317.
12. Saint Paul's exploration of the foolishness of idolatry in
Romans 1 appears to be heavily based on Wisdom 13.
13. McCarthy, "Exod. 3:14," 317. Cf. William Riordan, "Scriptural Ontology: The God of Abraham Is God the Plentitude
of Being," *Fellowship of Catholic Scholars Quarterly* 22, no. 3
(Summer 1999): 4–6.
14. McCarthy, "Exod. 3:14," 317 (emphasis in original).
15. Matthew Levering, *Scripture and Metaphysics: Aquinas and
the Renewal of Trinitarian Theology* (Malden, MA: Blackwell
Publishing, 2004), 63.
16. Yerushalmi Berakhot 9:5, in *The Talmud of the Land of
Israel: Berakhot*, vol. 1, ed. Jacob Neusner, trans. Tzvee Zahavy
(Chicago: University of Chicago Press, 1989), 343.
17. Mishnah Sanhedrin 10:1, in *Tractate Sanhedrin*, trans.
Herbert Danby (New York: MacMillan, 1919), 120. This
refusal to pronounce the divine name is also testified to by
the fourth-century Christian theologian Theodoret: "Among
the Hebrews this is known as the unspoken name; they are
forbidden to utter it aloud. It is written in four consonants,
and so they speak of it as the 'Tetragrammaton.' This name

was also inscribed on a plate of gold worn on the forehead of the high priest and bound to his head with a fillet." Theodoret, *The Questions on the Octateuch*, vol. 1, question 15 on Exodus, trans. Robert C. Hill (Washington, D.C.: Catholic University of America Press, 2007), 251.

18. There are nine times in 2 Samuel and 1 Kings in which the double title אדני יהוה (*Adonai YHWH*) appears (2 Sam 7:18, 19, 20, 22, 28, 29; 1 Kings 2:26, 8:53). In the parallel accounts in 1 Chronicles, each of these is changed to יהוה אלהים (*YHWH Elohim*) or simply יהוה (YHWH) (1 Chron 17:16, 17, 19, 20, 26, 27). Why? Koog P. Hong suggests it is due to "the practice of replacing יהוה with *Adonai*. As soon as יהוה is read as *Adonai*, this double title causes an awkward reading: *Adonai Adonai*." In other words, the author of 1 Chronicles anticipates that the text יהוה (YHWH) will be read as *Adonai*, suggesting that the Jewish practice of not speaking the Tetragrammaton is much older than is commonly assumed. Koog P. Hong, "The Euphemism for the Ineffable Name of God and Its Early Evidence in Chronicles," *Journal for the Study of the Old Testament*, 37, no. 4 (2013): 479, 482. This also points to a particularly vexing problem in tracing the history of Jewish praxis: if a Jewish reader was reading *YHWH* but saying *Adonai* (even in his own head!), there is seemingly no way to know whether the early Talmudic instruction to greet in the name of God meant greeting *YHWH* or *Adonai*.

19. John William Wevers, "The Rendering of the Tetragram in the Psalter and Pentateuch: A Comparative Study," in *The Old Greek Psalter: Studies in Honour of Albert Pietersma*, ed. Robert J. V. Hiebert, Claude E. Cox, and Peter J. Gentry (Sheffield, England: Sheffield Academic Press, 2001), 21–35.

20. Strangely, this refusal to say the divine name is how we ended up with the "name" *Jehovah* for God: to keep people from speaking the name, Jewish scribes didn't include the vowels in the name YHWH. Instead, they would mark the name with the vowels for *Adonai* (Lord). When Christians

mistakenly translated this, they got *Yehowah*, which eventually became *Jehovah*. See "Jehovah," in *The Jewish Encyclopedia*, vol. 7, 87. The linguistic shift from *Yehowah* to *Jehovah* is due to the fact that "a consistent distinction between both 'u' / 'v' and 'i' / 'j' did not come about until after the Renaissance." Lauree de Looze, *The Letter and The Cosmos* (Toronto, Canada: University of Toronto Press, 2016), 33.

21. Thomas Aquinas, *On the Two Commandments of Charity and the Ten Commandments of the Law*, trans. Henry Augustus Rawes (London: Burns and Oates, 1880), 95–101.

22. Luis de León, *The Names of Christ*, bk. 3, trans. Manuel Durán and William Kluback (New York: Paulist Press, 1984), 349.

23. Oliver Treanor, *Seven Bells to Bethlehem: The O Antiphons of Advent* (Leominster, England: Gracewing, 1995), 1.

24. Joseph Jensen, "The Age of Immanuel," *Catholic Biblical Quarterly* 41, no. 2 (April 1979): 220. See also Herbert M. Wolf, "A Solution to the Immanuel Prophecy in Isaiah 7:14–8:22," *Journal of Biblical Literature* 91, no. 4 (December 1972): 449: "The identification of Immanuel and his mother in Isa. 7:14 has been an object of heated debate for centuries. There is scarcely any other passage which has been subjected to so many varying analyses with regard to the translation of key words, the overall historical context, the nature of the passage, and its relation to ch. 8."

25. "Perhaps the most attractive option is that Immanuel and Maher-shalal-hash-baz were one and the same." John N. Oswalt, *The Book of Isaiah, Chapters 1–39* (Grand Rapids, MI: William B. Eerdmans, 1986), 213. See also Wolf, "A Solution to the Immanuel Prophecy," 449–56; Craig L. Blomberg, *Jesus and the Gospels: An Introduction and Survey*, 2nd ed. (Nashville: B and H Academic, 2009), 234; Hank Hanegraaff, *The Complete Bible Answer Book: Collector's Edition* (Nashville: Thomas Nelson, 2016).

26. Oswalt, *Book of Isaiah*, 221.

27. Otto Kaiser, *Isaiah 1–12*, 2nd English ed., trans. John Bowden (Philadelphia: Westminster Press, 1983), 160.

28. Warren W. Wiersbe, *The Bible Exposition Commentary: Old Testament Prophets* (Ontario, Canada: David C. Cook, 2002), 19.

29. The "most convincing" view interprets "the *almah* as a wife of King Ahaz and 'Immanuel' as an heir to the Davidic throne," and that "once we see the Immanuel child as a Davidic king, the *almah* would have been understood as a wife of King Ahaz." Edward P. Sri, *Queen Mother: A Biblical Theology of Mary's Queenship* (Steubenville, OH: Emmaus Road Publishing, 2005), 56–57.

30. Justin Martyr, "Dialogue with Trypho, 62," in *Ante-Nicene Fathers: Translations of the Writings of the Fathers Down to A.D. 325*, ed. Alexander Roberts and James Donaldson, vol. 1 (New York: Charles Scribner's Sons, 1905), 231.

31. Sanhedrin 94a, *The Babylonian Talmud*, vol. 3, ed. and trans. Isidore Epstein (London: Soncino Press, 1935). Several other instances of the Talmud presenting Hezekiah as a possible Messiah can be found in Song-Mi Suzie Park, *Hezekiah and the Dialogue of Memory* (Minneapolis: Fortress Press, 2015), 259.

32. The "coregency" interpretation of the text is the result of careful attention to biblical details in the books of 1 and 2 Kings and 1 and 2 Chronicles. It neatly harmonizes a great deal of apparently contradictory dating between these books (particularly when comparing the reigns of Judean and Samarian kings). The first to notice this pattern of coregency was Edwin R. Thiele in "Coregencies and Overlapping Reigns among the Hebrew Kings," *Journal of Biblical Literature* 93, no. 2 (June 1974): 174–200; the application of this to the reigns of Hezekiah and Ahaz (an oversight by Thiele) can be found in Leslie McFall, "Some Missing Coregencies in Thiele's Chronology," *Andrews University Seminary Studies* 30, no. 1 (1992): 35–58.

33. Michael Wilkins, "Apologetics Commentary on the Gospel

of Matthew," in *The Holman Apologetics Commentary on the Bible: The Gospels and Acts*, ed. Jeremy Royal Howard (Nashville: Holman Reference, 2013), 24.

34. "The most promising" interpretation is that "an unmarried young woman within the royal house will shortly marry and conceive" and that "her son would be called Immanuel ('God is with us')." "Proverbs–Isaiah," in *The Expositor's Bible Commentary*, vol. 6, ed. Tremper Longman III and David E. Garland (Grand Rapids, MI: Zondervan, 2008), 517.

35. J. Alec Motyer, *The Prophecy of Isaiah: An Introduction and Commentary* (Downers Grove, IL: InterVarsity Press, 1993), 85.

36. There were more than 2,500 boys named Emmanuel born in the United States in 2007 alone. Social Security Administration, "Popularity of Name Emmanuel," accessed December 3, 2019, https://www.ssa.gov/cgi-bin/babyname.cgi.

37. H. C. Ackerman, "The Immanuel Sign and Its Meaning," *The American Journal of Semitic Languages*, vol. 35 (Chicago, IL: University of Chicago Press, 1918), 208.

38. "Isaiah," in *Holman Concise Bible Commentary*, ed. David S. Dockery (Nashville: B and H Publishing Group, 2010), 267; Sri, *Queen Mother*, 56.

39. Abraham Lincoln, "Second Speech at Frederick, Maryland (October 4, 1862)," in *The Collected Works of Abraham Lincoln*, ed. Roy P. Basler, Marion Dolores Pratt, and Lloyd A. Dunlap, vol. 5 (New Brunswick, NJ: Rutgers University Press, 1953), 450.

40. Even the precise Hebrew wording used, *immānū*, is the root of *Immanuel*.

41. Benedict XVI, *Jesus of Nazareth: The Infancy Narratives*, trans. Philip J. Whitmore (New York: Image, 2012), 50.

42. The interpretation that Matthew is denying the perpetual virginity of Mary would be shocking to early Christians, who nearly universally believed in it. Many of these Christians also spoke Greek fluently, or at least far more fluently than the modern interpreters who claim that Matthew's use of *until*,

heōs (ἕως), implies that Joseph and Mary had sex after the birth of Christ. One the most famous of these early Christians is Saint Jerome (347–420), best known for having translated Scripture from Greek and Hebrew into Latin. When a man named Helvidius denied the perpetual virginity of Mary (in part, based on this passage in Matthew 1), ordinary Christians were taken aback and begged Jerome to respond. He eventually did so, around A.D. 383, saying: "I was requested by certain of the brethren not long ago to reply to a pamphlet written by one Helvidius. I have deferred doing so, not because it is a difficult matter to maintain the truth and refute an ignorant boor who has scarce known the first glimmer of learning, but because I was afraid my reply might make him appear worth defeating." "The Perpetual Virginity of Blessed Mary, Against Helvidius," in *Nicene and Post-Nicene Fathers*, 2nd series, vol. 6, *Jerome: Letters and Select Works*, ed. Philip Schaff and Rev. Henry Wallace (New York: Cosimo Classics, 2007), 335. It's worth noting Jerome's shock and disgust precisely because it gives us an indication precisely how far Helvidius's views were outside the mainstream of Christian orthodoxy in the fourth century.

43. In other words, if you want to understand the meaning of Matthew 1:25, you need to read it in the context of Matthew 1:22–23.

44. David K. Bernard, "The Future of Oneness Pentecostalism," in *The Future of Pentecostalism in the United States*, ed. Eric Patterson and Edmund John Rybarczyk (Lanham, MD: Lexington Books, 2007), 123–24.

45. Hein Kötz, *European Contract Law*, 2nd ed., trans. Gill Mertens and Tony Weir (Oxford, UK: Oxford University Press, 2017), 295.

46. Justin Harp, "Olly Murs actually forgot a girl's name while he was in the middle of a date with her," *Digital Spy*, September 15, 2016, accessed December 3, 2019, https://www.digitalspy .com/tv/a808083/olly-murs-forgot-a-girls-name-on-a-date/.

47. Timothy M. Dolan, *To Whom Shall We Go? Lessons from the Apostle Peter* (Huntington, IN: Our Sunday Visitor, 2008), 59.

Chapter 4

1. Karl Jaspers, *Socrates, Buddha, Confucius, Jesus: The Paradigmatic Individuals*, ed. Hannah Arendt, trans. Ralph Manheim (San Diego: Harcourt, Brace, 1962), 91.
2. Ibid., 83.
3. "Myth Versus Fact — The Truth about Jesus," *The Watchtower*, April 2010, accessed December 3, 2019, https://www.jw.org/en/publications/magazines/wp20100401/Myth-Versus-Fact-The-Truth-About-Jesus/.
4. "Why Jesus Was a Great Teacher," in *Learn from the Great Teacher*, website of the Jehovah's Witnesses, accessed December 3, 2019, https://www.jw.org/en/publications/books/learn-from-great-teacher-jesus/.
5. "I am trying here to prevent anyone saying the really foolish thing that people often say about Him: 'I'm ready to accept Jesus as a great moral teacher, but I don't accept his claim to be God.' That is the one thing we must not say. A man who was merely a man and said the sort of things Jesus said would not be a great moral teacher. He would either be a lunatic — on the level with the man who says he is a poached egg — or else he would be the Devil of Hell. You must make your choice. Either this man was, and is, the Son of God, or else a madman or something worse. You can shut him up for a fool, you can spit at him and kill him as a demon or you can fall at his feet and call him Lord and God, but let us not come with any patronising nonsense about his being a great human teacher. He has not left that open to us. He did not intend to." C. S. Lewis, *Mere Christianity* (New York: HarperOne, 2001), 52.
6. Ibid., 53.

7. For Islam, see Quran 33:50, ed Yasin T. al-Jibouri, trans. M. H. Shakir (Newington, VA: Yasin Publications, 2011), 374; Al-Tabari. As Muhammad's favorite wife, Aisha would later recount: "I was six years old when the Prophet married me and I was nine when he consummated the marriage. When he died, I was eighteen years old." *Ta'rikh*, 6:3201, 3222, quoted in Denise A. Spellberg, *Politics, Gender, and the Islamic Past: The Legacy of 'A'isha Bint Abi Bakr* (New York: Columbia University Press, 1994), 39. For Joseph Smith, see *The Doctrines and Covenants of the Church of Jesus Christ of Latter-Day Saints* (Salt Lake City: Church of Jesus Christ of Latter-Day Saints, 2013), 132, website of the Church of Jesus Christ of Latter-day Saints, accessed December 3, 2019, https://www.churchofjesuschrist.org/study/scriptures/dc -testament/title-page?lang=eng. By the end of his life, Smith was sexually involved with, and secretly "married to," some thirty-eight women, many of whom were still married to other men, all the while publicly denying that he believed in or taught polygamy. George Dempster Smith, *Nauvoo Polygamy: "... but We Called It Celestial Marriage"* (Salt Lake City: Signature Books, 2011). It was, as the March 1859 issue of the *Atlantic Monthly* described it, "a shameless lie." "The Utah Expedition: Its Causes and Consequences (Part I)," *Atlantic Monthly* (March 1859). For the Branch Davidians, see Gary Noesner, *Stalling for Time: My Life as an FBI Hostage Negotiator* (New York: Random House, 2018), 96. David Thibodeau, a former Branch Davidian, recounted how Koresh claimed that God had told him to "have a child with Michele, his wife's eleven-year-old sister," although he waited until after her twelfth birthday to begin sexual relations. David Thibodeau, with Leon Whiteson and Aviva Layton, *Waco: A Survivor's Story* (New York: Hachette Book Group, 2018), 103. Cf. Sara Rimer with Sam Howe Verhovek, "Growing Up under Koresh: Cult Children Tell of Abuses," *New York Times*, May 4, 1993, accessed December 3, 2019, https://www.nytimes

.com/1993/05/04/us/growing-up-under-koresh-cult-children-tell-of-abuses.html; James D. Tabor and Eugene V. Gallagher, *Why Waco? Cults and the Battle for Religious Freedom in America* (Berkeley, CA: University of California Press, 1995), 19.

8. Richard A. Gabriel, *Muhammad: Islam's First Great General* (Norman, OK: University of Oklahoma Press, 2007), 209.

9. Jon Krakauer, *Under the Banner of Heaven: A Story of Violent Faith* (New York: Anchor Books, 2004), 102. The accuracy of this sermon is disputed, because the source is an ex-Mormon by the name of Thomas B. Marsh. But Marsh isn't just any ex-Mormon. Shortly after Marsh was baptized a Mormon, Smith reported a divine revelation that Marsh would become "a physician unto the church." Eventually, Smith made him "President of the Quorum of the Twelve Apostles." In 1838, however, Marsh left the church, as he (according to the LDS church's own version of events) "was among several Latter-day Saints who became disturbed by the increasingly violent relationship between Church members and their Missouri neighbors." Kay Darowski, "The Faith and Fall of Thomas Marsh," in *Revelations in Context* (Salt Lake City: Church of Jesus Christ of Latter-day Saints, 2016), website of the Church of Jesus Christ of Latter-day Saints, accessed December 3, 2019, https://www.lds.org/manual/revelations-in-context/the-faith-and-fall-of-thomas-marsh.

10. Hamilton Gardner, "The Nauvoo Legion, 1840–1845: A Unique Military Organization," *Journal of the Illinois State Historical Society* 54, no. 2 (Summer 1961): 194–95.

11. Some have taken Saint Paul's mention of being able to take a "believing woman" (ἀδελφὴν γυναῖκα, *adelphēn gynaika*) as a reference to their having Christian wives. But in context, Paul is actually talking about how he and Barnabas have a right to material compensation, but that they forgo this right in order to avoid any hindrance to the Gospel (1 Cor 9:3–12). The "believing women" in question, then, are like those who

financially supported Jesus during his earthly ministry (Lk 8:1–3), and who appear to have done the same for Peter and the other apostles. Paul, in contrast, is a tent maker (Acts 18:3) and supports himself.

12. "Sanhedrin 43a," in *The William Davidson Talmud*, trans. Sefaria Community, Sefaria Library, accessed December 3, 2019, https://www.sefaria.org/Sanhedrin.43a.21.

13. Josh McDowell, *More Than a Carpenter* (Carol Stream, IL: Living Books, 2004), 57–58.

14. "Gittin 57a," in *The William Davidson Talmud*, trans. Sefaria Community, Sefaria Library, accessed December 3, 2019, https://www.sefaria.org/Gittin.57a.3.

15. Mark Shea, "Of the Making of Latest Real Jesuses There Is No End," *National Catholic Register*, December 24, 2010, accessed December 3, 2019, http://www.ncregister.com/blog/mark-shea/of-the-making-of-latest-real-jesuses-there-is-no-end.

16. Joseph Sievers, "Jesus of Nazareth as Seen by Jewish Writers of the XX Century," *Tertium Millenium*, no. 5 (November 1997), accessed December 3, 2019, http://www.vatican.va/jubilee_2000/magazine/documents/ju_mag_01111997_p-48_en.html.

17. Ibid.

18. Ibid.

19. Perhaps it's worth noting that this mode of biblical interpretation is nothing new. Martin Luther famously taught *sola fide*, the doctrine of justification by faith alone. Yet the only time the phrase appears in Scripture (excluding Luther's version of Romans 3:28, where he added it) is in James 2:24, which says "that a man is justified by works and not by faith alone." Luther's solution to this seemingly insurmountable problem was the same as that of these later scholars — simply wave away the evidence as a later addition. And so Luther claimed that the entire Epistle of James "is flatly against St. Paul and all the rest of Scripture in ascribing justification to

works," and that "this fault, therefore, proves that this epistle is not the work of any apostle." Martin Luther, *Prefaces to the New Testament*, trans. Charles M. Jacobs, Rev. E. Theodore Bachmann (Cabin John, MD: Wildside Press, 2010), 44–45. In other words, because Luther's interpretation of Saint Paul contradicts the Epistle of James, the Epistle of James must be wrong.

20. Charlie Jane Anders, "Is There Any Plausible Reason Why Aliens Would Evolve to Look Like Us?," *Gizmodo*, September 23, 2014, accessed December 3, 2019, https://io9.gizmodo .com/is-there-any-plausible-reason-why-aliens-would -evolve-t-1638235680.

21. Ibid.

22. Ronald Youngblood, *The Heart of the Old Testament: A Survey of Key Theological Themes*, 2nd ed. (Grand Rapids, MI: Baker Books, 1998), 12 (emphasis in original).

23. Saint Thomas Aquinas discusses this in greater detail in question 12 of the First Part of the *Summa Theologiae*, particularly in articles 7–8. The critical distinction is that "what is comprehended is perfectly known," and "it is clearly impossible for any created intellect to know God in an infinite degree."

24. Mark Konnert, *Early Modern Europe: The Age of Religious War, 1559–1715* (Toronto, Canada: Higher Education University of Toronto Press, 2008), 336.

25. Benedict XVI, "Faith, Reason and the University: Memories and Reflections," accessed December 3, 2019, Vatican.va. Wolfhart Pannenberg, "God of the Philosophers," *First Things,* June 2007, accessed December 3, 2019, https://www.firstthings .com/article/2007/06/002-god-of-the-philosophers.

26. As both the Anglican N. T. Wright and the Catholic Father (now Bishop) Robert Barron have noted, much of the biblical theology and scriptural commentary of the last two hundred years (Catholic and Protestant alike) has effectively divorced Jesus from his Judaism, severing and pitting against each other the Old and New Testaments. Barron notes that "if you look

back to Friedrich Schleiermacher [1768–1834], the founder of modern liberal Protestantism, follow Schleiermacher to people like [Albrecht] Ritschl, [Rudolph] Bultmann, [Karl] Rahner, [Paul] Tillich and David Tracy, what are you going to find? You are going to find a presentation of Jesus in which the Old Testament is never even mentioned. … For Schleiermacher, Jesus is the man with perfect God-consciousness. For Paul Tillich, Jesus is the one who experiences the new being. For Karl Rahner, Jesus is the one who is man in the presence of absolute mystery. For Bultmann, he's the man who utterly makes the right choice. The trouble is, Jesus has now been deracinated; he's been divorced from his Old Testament roots. It turns him into a bland cypher with no evangelical power." Robert Barron, "Six Suggestions about What Would Make the New Evangelization More Effective," Catholic Media Conference Opening Keynote Address, transcribed by the *Colorado Catholic Herald*, June 19, 2013, available online at https://www.catholicpress .org/resource/resmgr/2013_cmc/father_barron_transcription .docx. In contrast, argues Barron, the first evangelists recognized "that this Yeshua from Nazareth was the fulfillment of the expectation of Israel."

27. Jacob Neusner, *A Rabbi Talks with Jesus* (Montreal: McGill-Queen's University Press, 2000), 108.

28. Quoted in Dale Ahlquist, *Common Sense 101: Lessons from G. K. Chesterton* (San Francisco: Ignatius Press, 2006), 21.

29. Malcolm S. Salter, *Innovation Corrupted: The Origins and Legacy of Enron's Collapse* (Cambridge, MA: Harvard University Press, 2008), 306–7.

30. See Assnat Bartor, "Legal Texts," in *The Hebrew Bible: A Critical Companion*, ed. John Barton (Princeton, NJ: Princeton University Press, 2016), 168.

31. "The apostasies of Sinai only served to remind the nation why Yahweh had given them the Mosaic legislation. They needed standards. Without the order those standards produced, there would be chaos and anarchy. The nation must be

prepared for their landed inheritance. Israel received the legal stipulations of the Mosaic Covenant to prepare them for living in the promised land." William D. Barrick, "The Mosaic Covenant," *Master's Seminary Journal* 10, no. 2 (Fall 1999): 228.

32. Israel Drazin, "There Are Not 613 Biblical Commands," *Times of Israel*, May 31, 2017, accessed December 3, 2019, https://blogs.timesofisrael.com/there-are-not-613-biblical-commands/.

33. *Babylonian Talmud Makkot* 24A-B.

34. Neusner, *A Rabbi Talks with Jesus*, 107–8.

35. Luis de León, *The Names of Christ*, bk. 3, trans. Manuel Durán and William Kluback (New York: Paulist Press, 1984), 349.

36. Erasmo Leiva-Merikakis, *Fire of Mercy, Heart of the Word: Meditations on the Gospel according to Matthew*, vol. 3 (San Francisco: Ignatius Press, 2012), 351n5.

37. McCarthy, "Exod. 3:14," 317.

38. Erasmo Leiva-Merikakis, *Fire of Mercy, Heart of the Word: Meditations on the Gospel according to Matthew*, vol. 1 (San Francisco: Ignatius Press, 1996), 70.

39. Leiva-Merikakis, *Fire of Mercy*, 3:351n5.

Chapter 5

1. Smith, Doctrines and Covenants 130:22, accessed December 3, 2019, https://www.lds.org/study/scriptures/dc-testament/dc/130.22.

2. Church of Jesus Christ of Latter-day Saints, "God, Body of, Corporeal Nature," *Topical Guide*, website of the Church of Jesus Christ of Latter-day Saints, accessed December 3, 2019, https://www.lds.org/scriptures/tg/god-body-of-corporeal-nature.

3. Philo, *De opificio mundi*, par. 69, quoted in Walter J. Burghardt, *The Image of God in Man according to Cyril of Alexandria* (Eugene, OR: Wipf and Stock, 2009), 12.

4. Ibid.

5. Ibid., 12–13.

6. Athanasius, *On the Incarnation: The Treatise De Incarnatione Verbi Dei*, trans. Sr. Penelope Lawson (Crestwood, NY: St. Vladmir's Seminary Press, 1993), 28.

7. It's a fitting insight from a man named Athanasius, meaning "immortal" or "deathless." It's a negation of *Thanos*, "death."

8. Saint John Damascene, *On Holy Images*, trans. Mary H. Allies (London: Thomas Baker, 1898), 11.

9. Ibid., 10.

10. Harry Torczyner, *Magritte, Ideas and Images*, trans. Richard Miller (New York: Harry N. Abrams, 1977), 118.

11. The earliest Desert Fathers, including Saint Antony of the Desert (A.D. c. 251–356), began this way of life prior to the legalization of Christianity, but it became more popular after the Edict of Milan and the Christianization of the Roman Empire. "It should seem to us stranger than it does, this paradoxical flight from the world that attained its greatest dimensions (I almost said frenzy) when the 'world' became officially Christian. ... They seem to have doubted that Christianity and politics could ever be mixed to such an extent as to produce a fully Christian society." Thomas Merton, *The Wisdom of the Desert: Sayings from the Desert Fathers of the Fourth Century* (New York: New Directions, 1960), 3–4. For an excellent biography of Saint Antony, told by another great Saint, I recommend *The Life of Antony*, written by his contemporary Saint Athanasius.

12. Quoted in Merton, *The Wisdom of the Desert*, 76.

13. Sasha Adkins, *From Disposable Culture to Disposable People: The Unintended Consequences of Plastics* (Eugene, OR: Resource Publications, 2018), 56.

14. Peter Leithart, "De-Fragmenting Modernity," *Patheos*, August 9, 2018, accessed December 3, 2019, https://www.patheos.com/blogs/leithart/2018/08/de-fragmenting-modernity/.

15. Robin A. Parry, *The Biblical Cosmos: A Pilgrim's Guide to the Weird and Wonderful World of the Bible* (Eugene, OR: Cas-

cade Books, 2014), 159.

16. Carl Sagan, *Pale Blue Dot: A Vision of the Human Future in Space* (New York: Ballantine Books, 1994), 6–7. Sagan notes that this observation is not an original one. The Roman emperor Marcus Aurelius, in his *Meditations*, had said back in A.D. 170 that "the entire Earth is but a point, and the place of our own habitation but a minute corner of it." Quoted in Sagan, *Pale Blue Dot*, 1.

17. John Paul II, "By the Communion of Persons Man Becomes the Image of God," General Audience (November 14, 1979), accessed December 3, 2019, http://w2.vatican.va/.

18. Ibid.

19. Michael Guinan, *Gospel Poverty: Witness to the Risen Christ* (New York: Paulist Press, 1981), 78.

20. Augustine, "On the Holy Trinity," bk. 15, chap. 17, par. 27, in *Nicene and Post-Nicene Fathers*, 1st series, vol. 3, *Augustine: On the Trinity, Doctrinal Treatises, Moral Treatises*, ed. Philip Schaff (Buffalo, NY: Christian Literature, 1887), 215.

21. Ronald Knox, *On the Belief of Catholics* (San Francisco: Ignatius Press, 2000), 161.

22. *The Order of Celebrating Matrimony*, quoted in Perry J. Cahall, *The Mystery of Marriage: A Theology of the Body and the Sacrament* (Chicago: Hillenbrand Books, 2014), 61.

23. Leon Kass, *The Hungry Soul: Eating and the Perfecting of Our Nature* (Chicago: University of Chicago Press, 1999), 50.

24. Ibid.

25. Arne Kislenko, *Culture and Customs of Thailand* (Westport, CT: Greenwood Press, 2004), 153.

26. One of the first things the rebels did in their attempted break from Rome was to create currency "Jerusalem the Holy," with an image of the Temple on the other. Jerome Murphy-O'Connor, "Jesus and the Money Changers (Mark 11:15–17, John 2:13–17)," *Revue Biblique* 107, no. 1 (January 2000): 47. Murphy-O'Connor corrects a popular Christian misconception that the moneychangers in the Temple area

were there to transfer " 'secular' coins bearing royal images into aniconic 'holy' coins." In fact, since the Jews had no mint of their own and refused to use Roman coins in the Temple for the national sacrifice, they were forced to use coins from nearby Tyre bearing the head of the false god Melkart on one side and the inscription "Tyre the holy and inviolable" on the obverse. The coins minted by the Jewish rebels seem designed as an intentional contrast from that humiliation.

27. "Veni Creator Spiritus," trans. Adrian Fortescue, posted on Corpus Christi Watershed, accessed December 3, 2019, http://www.ccwatershed.org/media/pdfs/15/05/21/22-27-02_0.pdf.

Chapter 6

1. John Piper, "How to Become a Child of God," *Desiring God,* December 17, 1989, accessed December 3, 2019, https://www.desiringgod.org/messages/how-to-become-a-child-of-god.

2. As Saint Gregory Nazianzen preached in a homily in 381, Jesus comes to the Jordan "to bury the whole of the old Adam in the water; and before this and for the sake of this, to sanctify Jordan; for as He is Spirit and Flesh, so He consecrates us by Spirit and water." Oration 39, trans. Charles Gordon Browne and James Edward Swallow, in *Nicene and Post-Nicene Fathers,* 2nd series, vol. 7, *Cyril of Jerusalem, Gregory Nazianzen,* ed. Philip Schaff (New York: Christian Literature, 1894), 357.

3. Charlton T. Lewis and Charles Short, "Prōdĭgus," in *A Latin Dictionary: Founded on Andrews' Edition of Freund's Latin Dictionary* (Oxford: Trustees of Tufts University, 1879), 1455.

4. "This is true humility: not thinking less of ourselves but thinking of ourselves *less.*" Rick Warren, *The Purpose-Driven Life* (Grand Rapids, MI: Zondervan, 2002), 265 (emphasis in original). Christians often imagine that humility is pretending to be worse than you really are. But this false self-abasement is still fixated on ourselves. Instead, as Saint Augustine counsels, we must turn away from ourselves toward God: "Let us

remember that we shouldn't have too much confidence in ourselves. Let us entrust God with whatever good qualities we have; what we have rather less of, let us implore from him." Sermon 285, in *The Works of St. Augustine*, vol. 3, ed. John E. Rotelle, trans. Edmund Hill (Hyde Park, NY: New City Press, 1994), 97–98.

5. Based on the ambiguous construction of Judges 7:5–7, there are several contradictory readings of the text, with some modern exegetes reading in it the opposite of what I have described. These readings tend to ignore the crucial detail of the canine imagery. "The comparison to the dog merits closer scrutiny. Some scholars virtually ignore the reference, assuming that it serves merely to emphasize the act of lapping water with the tongue." Aaron Hornkohl, "Resolving the Crux of Judges 7:5B7: A Critique of Two Traditional Approaches and the Reproposal of a Third," *Hebrew Studies* 50 (2009): 81. Hornkohl relies on medieval Jewish exegetes to distinguish between the " 'dog-like' lappers of verse 5a" and " 'hand-using' lappers of verses 6a and 7a," and observes that "Gideon is instructed to set apart those who get down on all fours and lap like dogs." It's through these odd men that God works the victory over the Midianites.

6. Bruce Feiler, "For the Love of Being 'Liked,' " *New York Times*, May 9, 2014, accessed December 3, 2019, https://www .nytimes.com/2014/05/11/fashion/for-some-social-media -users-an-anxiety-from-approval-seeking.html.

7. Greg Lukianoff and Jonathan Haidt, *The Coddling of the American Mind* (New York: Penguin Press, 2018), 149.

8. Jean M. Twenge, *iGen: Why Today's Super-Connected Kids Are Growing Up Less Rebellious, More Tolerant, Less Happy — and Completely Unprepared for Adulthood* (New York: Atria Books, 2017), 102.

9. Liu yi Lin, Jaime E. Sidani, Ariel Shensa, Ana Radovic, Elizabeth Miller, Jason B. Colditz, Beth L. Hoffman, Leila M Giles, and Brian A. Primack, "Association between Social

Media Use and Depression among U.S. Young Adults," author's manuscript, *HHS Public Access,* available online at https://www.ncbi.nlm.nih.gov/pmc/articles/PMC4853817/. Final published form available in *Depression and Anxiety* 33, no. 4 (April 2016): 323–31.

10. "Social Media Use Increases Depression and Loneliness, Study Finds," *Science Daily*, November 8, 2018, accessed December 3, 2019, https://www.sciencedaily.com/releases/2018/11/181108164316.htm.

11. Melissa G. Hunt, Rachel Marx, Courtney Lipson, and Jordyn Young, "No More FOMO: Limiting Social Media Decreases Loneliness and Depression," *Journal of Social and Clinical Psychology* 37, no. 10 (2018): 763, posted at Guilford Press, accessed December 3, 2019, https://guilfordjournals.com/doi/10.1521/jscp.2018.37.10.751.

12. Why, then, do we not always get what we want in prayer? Paul explains that although we are heirs, we've not yet reached the age of maturity, and "the heir, as long as he is a child, is no better than a slave, though he is the owner of all the estate; but he is under guardians and trustees until the date set by the father" (Gal 4:1–2). In modern terms, we might speak of a trust fund, which parents create for their children to inherit upon reaching a certain age. Only here, the trust fund is the entire estate. We are still juveniles, so we don't presently exercise any great control over heaven and earth. But the divine promise is right there, plain as day. Because the Father's promise is that "all that I have is yours," Saint Paul refers to the Christian as "the owner of all the estate," simply awaiting the "date set by the Father" to inherit all things. Why the wait? Because we are still juveniles, certain restrictions are in place. This is the whole reason a trust fund exists: because the law is aware that young children shouldn't be entrusted with fortunes. Without some sort of oversight, some protection from their own worse impulses, they would spend it frivolously. And so, unfortunately, do we.

Chapter 7

1. Alex Williams, "Baby Names That Shout Out 'I Am … ,' "
New York Times, May 31, 2013, accessed December 3, 2019,
https://nytimes.com/2013/06/02/fashion/the-new-baby-name
-anxiety.html.
2. Carlton F. W. Larson, "Naming Baby: The Constitutional
Dimensions of Parental Naming Rights," *George Washington
Law Review* 80, no. 1 (November 2011): 162.
3. Polly Mosendz, "You Can Now Pay Someone to Name Your
Baby," *Bloomberg*, April 19, 2016, accessed December 3, 2019,
https://www.bloomberg.com/news/articles/2016-04-19/you-
can-now-pay-someone-to-name-your-baby. Cf. Alexandra
Alter, "The Baby-Name Business," *Wall Street Journal*, June 22,
2007, accessed December 3, 2019, https://www.wsj
.com/articles/SB118247444843644288 (tracing the growth of
the baby-naming industry from the mid-'90s to 2007). This
growth has only escalated since then, with the proliferation of
online resources related to baby naming. Caroline Bologna,
"How Technology Is Changing Baby Names," *Huffington Post*,
December 21, 2018, accessed December 3, 2019, https://www
.huffpost.com/entry/technology-baby-names-influence
_n_5c096ad6e4b0de79357ad871.
4. David N. Figlio, "Boys Named Sue: Disruptive Children and
Their Peers," *Education Finance and Policy* 2, no. 4 (Fall 2007):
376–94.
5. David N. Barton and Jamin Halberstadt, "A Social Bouba/
Kiki Effect: A Bias for People Whose Names Match Their
Faces," *Psychonomic Bulletin and Review* 25, no. 3 (June 2018):
1013–20. The authors note that participants across a wide variety of cultures and languages "almost unanimously matched
curvy shapes with the novel word 'bouba' and angular shapes
with the novel word 'kiki.' "
6. Ibid.
7. Margo DeMello, *Animals and Society: An Introduction to
Human-Animal Studies* (New York: Columbia University Press,

2012), 148–49.

8. Ibid., 130.

9. Marc Bekoff, *The Animal Manifesto: Six Reasons for Expanding Our Compassion Footprint* (Novato, CA: New World Library, 2010), 109.

10. Ben Sasse, *Them: Why We Hate Each Other — and How to Heal* (New York: St. Martin's Press, 2018), 61.

11. John Paul II, "The Meaning of Man's Original Solitude," accessed December 3, 2019, vatican.va.

12. Albert Einstein, *Out of My Later Years* (New York: Citadel Press, 1984), 5.

13. G. K. Chesterton, *The Everlasting Man* (Mineola, NY: Dover Publications, 2007), 13.

14. Kass, *The Hungry Soul*, 118.

15. Matthew Henry, *An Exposition of All the Books of the Old and New Testaments*, vol. 1 (London: W. Lochhead, 1804), 12.

16. John Dewey and Arthur F. Bentley, *Knowing and the Known* (Boston: Beacon Press, 1949), 147.

17. Ludwig Wittgenstein, *Philosophical Investigations*, trans. G. E. M. Anscombe (Oxford: Basil Blackwell, 1986), 81, par. 202. For more on this debate, see Saul Kripke, *Wittgenstein on Rules and Private Language: An Elementary Exposition* (Cambridge, MA: Harvard University Press, 1982).

18. Lewis Carroll, *Alice's Adventures in Wonderland* and *Through the Looking-Glass* (New York: Cosimo Classics, 2010), 57.

19. Ibid., 58. In *Obergefell v. Hodges*, the Supreme Court declared the "the right to marry is fundamental because it supports a two-person union unlike any other in its importance to the committed individuals." But despite declaring a constitutional right for two men or two women (but, for some reason, no more than two) to marry, the Court never defined what "marriage" is. "Since the dawn of history, marriage has transformed strangers into relatives, binding families and societies together," the Court pontificated, before quickly conceding that "it is fair and necessary to say these references were

based on the understanding that marriage is a union between two persons of the opposite sex." So all through history, people have rightly recognized that marriage is great, but it turns out, they didn't know what marriage is. That's a Humpty Dumpty approach to language if ever there was one: take a word you like the sound of, and apply it to whatever you'd like. But even Humpty Dumpty had the humility to explain his unique meanings of words to Alice.

20. Such cases do occur, perhaps most famously that of the Olympic gold medalist Picabo Street, who named herself at the age of three (although her mother had nicknamed her Peek-a-boo earlier) after being listed as "Baby Girl Street" on her birth certificate. She now has a "love / hate relationship" with her "given" name. Picabo Street and Dana White, *Picabo: Nothing to Hide* (Chicago: Contemporary Books, 2002), 24.

21. Larson, "Naming Baby," 185.

22. Fabien Perrin, Luis García-Larrea, François Mauguière, and Hélène Bastuji, "A Differential Brain Response to the Subject's Own Name Persists During Sleep," *Clinical Neurophysiology* 110, no. 12 (December 1, 1999): 2153–64.

23. Helen Keller, *The Story of My Life* (Jangpura, India: Madhubun, 2015), 23.

24. Ibid., 24.

25. Ibid.

26. F. J. Sheed, *To Know Christ Jesus* (Mansfield Centre, CT: Martino Publishing, 2016), 148.

27. Sheed, 148.

28. John F. MacArthur, *MacArthur New Testament Commentary*, vol. 3 (Chicago: Moody Publishers, 1988), 18; George Martin, *The Gospel according to Mark: Meaning and Message* (Chicago: Loyola Press, 2005), 201, 218; John Kitto, *The Popular Cyclopaedia of Biblical Literature: Condensed from the Larger Work* (Boston: Gould and Lincoln, 1852), 167.

29. "Son of" is often used in such a nonbiological sense (for instance, *bar mitzvah* literally means "son of the law").

30. John Paul II, *Fides et Ratio*.

31. David C. Scott, *Re-Envisioning Transformation: Toward a Theology of the Christian Life* (Eugene, OR: Wipf and Stock, 2018), 85 (describing the theology of Saint Maximus the Confessor).

32. "Strictly speaking, the 'Christian name' is not merely the forename distinctive of the individual member of a family, but the name given to him at his 'christening,' i.e., his baptism." Herbert Thurston, "Christian Names," *Catholic Encyclopedia*, vol. 10 (New York: Robert Appleton Company, 1911), 673.

33. The third-century patriarch Saint Dionysius of Alexandria referred to this when he said, "I am of the opinion that there were many with the same name as the apostle John, who, on account of their love for him, and because they admired and emulated him, and desired to be loved by the Lord as he was, took to themselves the same surname, as many of the children of the faithful are called Paul or Peter." Eusebius, "Church History," bk. 7, 25, trans. Arthur Cushman McGiffert (Oxford: Parker and Company, 1890) in *Nicene and Post-Nicene Fathers*, 2nd series, vol. 1, *Eusebius: Church History from A.D. 1–324, Life of Constantine the Great, Oration in Praise of Constantine*, ed. Philip Schaff and Rev. Henry Wallace (New York: Cosimo, 2007), 310.

34. Otto Erich Deutsch, *Mozart: A Documentary Biography*, trans. Eric Blom, Peter Branscombe, and Jeremy Noble (Stanford, CA: Stanford University Press, 1966), 95.

35. Claire Cain Miller and Derek Willis, "Maiden Names, on the Rise Again," *New York Times*, June 27, 2015, accessed December 3, 2019, nytimes.com/2015/06/28/upshot /maiden-names-on-the-rise-again.html (finding that only about "20 percent of women married in recent years have kept their names").

36. Mark Memmot, "5 Things about Popes and Their Names; Like, Why Do They Change Them?," *NPR*, March 12, 2013, accessed December 3, 2019, https://www.npr.org/sections

/thetwo-way/2013/03/12/174108843/5-things-about-popes
-and-their-names-like-why-do-they-change-them (noting that
the last pope to use his baptismal name was Marcellus II in
1555).

37. Some Christians will tell you that Peter's name means "little rock" or "pebble," but that's not true. We know from John
1:42 that the name Jesus gives to Simon is *Kefa* (כֵּיפָא, kēp̄ā'),
an Aramaic word that means simply "rock." Even in Greek, we
know from works such as the third-century-B.C. *Argonautica*
that *petros* was used to describe huge boulders. The reason Jesus' word is translated as *petros* instead of *petra* here is because
petra is a female name.

38. John Calvin, *Institutes of Christian Religion*, vol. 3, bk. 4,
trans. Henry Beveridge (Edinburgh: Calvin Translation Society, 1846), 155.

39. See Joe Heschmeyer, "St. Peter: Rock or Stumbling-Stone?"
Catholic Answers, February 21, 2018, accessed December 3,
2019, https://www.catholic.com/magazine/online-edition
/st-peter-rock-or-stumbling-stone.

40. Joseph Ratzinger, "Freimut und Gehorsam," in *Das Neue
Volk Gottes* (Düsseldorf: Patmos-Verlag, 1969) 249–66; an
English translation, "Sincerity and Obedience," is found in
Heinrich Fries, *Fundamental Theology*, trans. Robert J. Daly
(Washington, D.C.: Catholic University of America Press,
1985), 473.

41. Ratzinger, "Freimut und Gehorsam," 258–59, in Fries, *Fundamental Theology*, 474.

42. Ambrose, "On the Mysteries," 49, trans. H. De Romestin, in
Nicene and Post-Nicene Fathers, 2nd series, vol. 10, *Ambrose:
Select Works and Letters*, ed. Philip Schaff and Rev. Henry
Wace (New York: Christian Literature, 1896), 323.

43. Francis de Sales, *Treatise on the Love of God*, trans. Henry
Benedict Mackey (Rockford, IL: TAN Books and Publishers,
1997), 233.

44. Scott, *Re-Envisioning Transformation*, 85 (describing the

theology of Saint Maximus the Confessor).

45. Thomas Aquinas, *Summa Theologiae*, I-II, q.94, a.2, trans. Fathers of the English Dominican Province (New York: Benziger Brothers, 1915), 43. Cf. J. Budziszewski, *Commentary on Thomas Aquinas's Treatise on Law Book* (New York: Cambridge University Press, 2014), 244.

46. Mind you, this doesn't excuse sin. The point here is simply that even when you do evil, part of you inescapably wants to be doing good.

47. Bruce Marshall, *The World, the Flesh, and Father Smith* (Garden City, NY: Image Books, 1957), 114.

48. "Transcript: Tom Brady, Part 3," *Sixty Minutes*, June 2005, December 3, 2019, https://www.cbsnews.com/news/transcript -tom-brady-part-3/.

49. Francis, *Evangelii Gaudium*, accessed December 3, 2019, Vatican.va, par. 265.

50. Augustine, *Confessions*, bk. 1, trans. J. G. Pilkington (Edinburgh, UK: T & T Clark, 1876), 1.

51. Pliny the Elder, *The Natural History of Pliny*, vol. 2, trans. John Bostock and H. T. Riley (London: Henry G. Bohn, 1855), 434.

52. Francis de Sales, *Treatise on the Love of God*, 82.

53. Luigi Giussani, *Why the Church?*, trans. Viviane Hewitt (Montreal: McGill-Queen's University Press, 2001), 219–20.

54. Francis, *Gaudete et Exsultate*, accessed December 3, 2019, Vatican.va, par. 34.

55. For an example of the misquotation, see James Martin, "To Be a Saint, Just Be Who You Are," *America*, February 8, 2019.

56. "Letter CCLXXXIX (June 10, 1605)," in Francis de Sales and Jane de Chantal, *Letters of Spiritual Direction*, trans. Peronne Marie Thibert, VHM, ed. Wendy M. Wright and Joseph F. Power, OSFS (New York: Paulist Press, 1988), 111.

57. Ibid.

Chapter 8

1. Johannes Jørgensen, *Saint Catherine of Siena*, trans. Ingeborg Lund (Eugene, OR: Wipf and Stock, 2012), 48 (emphasis in original).
2. Julian Baggini, *Atheism: A Brief Insight* (New York: Sterling, 2009), 57–58.
3. Walter Sinnott-Armstrong, *Morality without God?* (Oxford: Oxford University Press, 2009), 45–46.
4. Ibid., 47.
5. Richard Dawkins, *The God Delusion* (New York: Mariner Books, 2008), 356 (emphasis in original).
6. Ibid., 357–58.
7. Third Plenary Council of Baltimore, *A Manual of Prayers: For the Use of the Catholic Laity* (New York: Catholic Publication Society, 1889), 286.
8. Blaise Pascal, *Pensées*, trans. W. F. Trotter (Mineola, NY: Dover Publications, 2003), 113.
9. Augustine, *Confessions*, bk. 1, chap. 1.
10. Gail Dines, "Is Porn Immoral? That Doesn't Matter: It's a Public Health Crisis," *Washington Post*, April 8, 2016, accessed December 3, 2019, https://www.washingtonpost.com /posteverything/wp/2016/04/08/is-porn-immoral-that -doesnt-matter-its-a-public-health-crisis/.
11. See W. James Popham, "Teaching to the Test?," *Educational Leadership* 58, no. 6 (March 2001): 16–20, accessed December 3, 2019, http://www.ascd.org/publications/educational -leadership/mar01/vol58/num06/Teaching-to-the -Test%C2%A2.aspx.
12. Thomas Aquinas, *Summa Theologiae*, II-II, q.19, a.10.
13. Pope Leo I, "Sermon 21," in *St. Leo the Great Sermons,* trans. Jane Patricia Freeland and Agnes Josephine Conway (Washington, D.C.: Catholic University of America Press, 1996), 79.
14. David Frost, *Billy Graham: Candid Conversations with a Public Man* (Colorado Springs, CO: David C. Cook, 2014), 176.

15. The god of our universe lives near the planet (or star) Kolob, according to Joseph Smith. Abraham 3:2–3.

16. The first quotation is 2 Peter 1:4. It is followed by quotations from Saint Irenaeus, Saint Athanasius, and Saint Thomas Aquinas.

17. Athanasius, "Discourse III against the Arians," chap. 15, 19, trans. J. H. Newman and Archibald Robinson, in *Nicene and Post-Nicene Fathers*, 2nd series, vol. 4, *The Anti-Manichaean Writings, The Anti-Donatist Writings*, ed. Philip Schaff and Rev. Henry Wace (New York: Cosimo, 2007), 404.

18. Ibid.

19. Aristotle, *Nicomachean Ethics*, bk. 10, chap. 8, trans. C. D. C. Reeve (Indianapolis, IN: Hackett Publishing, 2014), 188.

20. From a letter of Saint Clare of Assisi to Blessed Agnes of Prague, used in the Roman Office of Readings for the feast of Saint Clare, August 11.

21. "A Spiritual Canticle between the Soul and Christ" in *The Complete Works of Saint John of the Cross*, trans. David Lewis, vol. 2 (London: Longman, Green, Longman, Roberts, and Green, 1864), 197.

22. Joint Commission for Theological Dialogue between the Roman Catholic Church and the Orthodox Church, "The Mystery of the Church and of the Eucharist in the Light of the Mystery of the Holy Trinity," accessed December 3, 2019, Vatican.va, par. 4b.

23. "On the Priesthood," bk. 3, chap. 4, in *Nicene and Post-Nicene Fathers*, 1st series, vol. 9, *St. Chrysostom: On the Priesthood; Ascetic Treatises; Select Homilies and Letters; Homilies on the Statutes*, ed. Philip Schaff (New York: Christian Literature, 1889), 46.

24. Francis, *Gaudete et Exsultate*, pars. 19, 20.

25. C. S. Lewis, *The Weight of Glory: And Other Addresses* (New York: HarperOne, 2001), 45 (emphasis in original).

26. Ibid., 45–46.

Conclusion

1. Dennis Coon and John O. Mitterer, *Introduction to Psychology: Gateways to Mind and Behavior,* 12th ed. (Belmont, CA: Cengage Learning, 2010), 37.
2. Jason G. Goldman, "Know the Jargon: 'Human Shield Effect,' " *Scientific American,* October 1, 2014, accessed December 3, 2019, https://www.scientificamerican.com/article/know-the-jargon -human-shield-effect/.
3. Weizmann Institute of Science, "Quantum Theory Demonstrated: Observation Affects Reality," *ScienceDaily,* February 27, 1998, accessed December 3, 2019. https:// www.sciencedaily.com/releases/1998/02/980227055013.htm. Cf. Daniel Greenberger, Klaus Hentschel, and Friedel Weinert, eds., *Compendium of Quantum Physics: Concepts, Experiments, History and Philosophy* (Dordrecht, Netherlands: Springer, 2009).
4. Thomas Aquinas, *Summa Theologiae,* I, q.12, a.6–7.
5. *Story of a Soul: The Autobiography of St. Therese of Lisieux,* 3rd ed., trans. John Clarke (Washington, D.C.: ICS Publications, 2017), 45.
6. Augustine of Hippo, *Tractates on the Gospel of John 112–24; Tractates on the First Epistle of John,* trans. John W. Rettig (Washington, D.C.: Catholic University of America Press, 1995), 179.

About the Author

Once a litigator in Washington, D.C., and then a seminarian for the Archdiocese of Kansas City, Joe Heschmeyer now works as an instructor for the Holy Family School of Faith Institute, helping people to grow in friendship with Jesus Christ and with one another through ongoing one-on-one discipleship, small gatherings, and large-group formation. His writing has appeared in *Catholic Answers Magazine*, the *Washington Times*, *Word on Fire*, *First Things*, and *Strange Notions*. In 2014, he was named one of FOCUS's "30 Under 30." He cohosts *The Catholic Podcast* weekly and has run the blog *Shameless Popery* since 2009. Joe lives in Overland Park, Kansas, with his wife, Anna, and their daughter, Stella Maris.

A God Who Questions

"Where are you?" God called out to the first couple in the Garden of Eden. He never stops asking us the same question.

The divine search for us continues in the person of Jesus Christ, the Word of God made flesh. When Jesus himself asks questions in the New Testament, he asks not because he needs an answer, but to draw us out of the shadows and into his presence. And he asks a lot of questions:

"Do you want to be healed?"

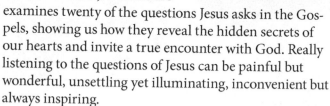

"Who do the crowds say that I am?"

"Why do you call me good?"

"Whom do you seek?"

In **A God Who Questions**, author Leonard J. DeLorenzo examines twenty of the questions Jesus asks in the Gospels, showing us how they reveal the hidden secrets of our hearts and invite a true encounter with God. Really listening to the questions of Jesus can be painful but wonderful, unsettling yet illuminating, inconvenient but always inspiring.

T2207

OSVCatholicBookstore.com or wherever books are sold.

A Life of Conversion

"As Jesus passed on from there, he saw a man called Matthew sitting at the tax office; and he said to him, 'Follow me.' And he rose and followed him." — Matthew 9:9

Conversion. The word is often associated with a one-time event, such as the call of Saint Matthew. But even for Matthew, that call was only the beginning, the moment when he started following Jesus. For Matthew, as for all the saints, his conversion lasted a lifetime. Real conversion — repentance and turning toward God — is a process that happens daily. It is our continual "yes" to the Lord and the grace he offers us.

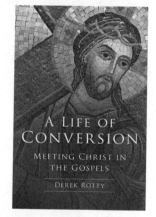

In **A Life of Conversion**, Derek Rotty walks through eight Gospel passages that reveal essential lessons about conversion. Through these stories from Scripture, you will encounter Christ again and again, and, with him as your model, you'll be drawn into a deeper relationship with the master of conversion.

Each chapter includes reflection questions that are perfect for both individual and group study.

T2017

OSVCatholicBookstore.com or wherever books are sold.